D0331636

98%
Funky Stuff

Copyright © 2013 by Maceo Parker
First edition
Published by Chicago Review Press, Incorporated
814 North Franklin Street
Chicago, Illinois 60610

ISBN 978-1-61374-346-1

Interior design: PerfecType, Nashville, TN

Library of Congress Cataloging-in-Publication Data
Parker, Maceo.
  98% funky stuff : my life in music / Maceo Parker. — 1st ed.
     p. cm.
  Includes index.
  ISBN 978-1-61374-346-1 (hardcover)
1. Parker, Maceo. 2. Saxophonists—United States—Biography. I. Title. II.
Title: Ninety-eight percent funky stuff.

ML419.P367A3 2013
 788.7'164092—dc23
 [B]

                                2012037923

Printed in the United States of America
5 4 3 2 1

Contents

Preface

You're Gonna Know Me

It's the fall of 1963, and I'm nineteen years old. I'm standing out back of the Coliseum in Greensboro, North Carolina, during intermission, trying to catch a glimpse of my idol, Ray Charles. I've just seen him play an incredible set with his band, and I'm certain they've come out back for some air. I walk around searching the faces in the throng of people milling about, looking for anyone in the band—David "Fathead" Newman, Philip Guilbeau, Marcus Belgrave, Edgar Willis, Bruno Carr. I would recognize any one of them instantly, but all I see are strangers. I'm not entirely sure what I'll do when I find them, but I feel an irresistible pull to them. I want to see them. I want to see Ray.

Out of the corner of my eye I notice the flare of a lighter. Someone is lighting a cigarette. I turn my head and instantly know who it is. Leaned up against a pole is Ray's alto player, Hank Crawford. He's the absolute epitome of cool in his leather jacket and matching boots. It's nearly midnight, but he still has his sunglasses on. I stand in the shadows for what seems like an eternity, watching as he takes long drags of his cigarette, not sure if I should approach him or not. I wouldn't know what to say if I did, but I've been enamored with his playing ever since I heard "What'd I Say." I love his sound, his phrasing.

It's the fall of my junior year in college, and I'm feeling an increasing pull away from school, away from the life of a music teacher and toward the kind of life that Hank leads. I want to be out on the road in an incredible band, playing packed houses every night. I know deep down that the life of a teacher is not for me. There's something else inside that's dying to get out.

The back door of the Coliseum opens, and the rest of the band spills out. They gather around, laughing and talking, occasionally speaking to some of the other people who've been waiting to see them.

Then Ray Charles himself emerges. I'm completely awestruck. I'm close enough to walk over and touch him. I want to say something, but I know anything I say will sound like the ramblings of just another star-struck fan. My admiration for this man and his music goes so much deeper than that. When I introduce myself to Hank Crawford, David Newman, and especially Ray Charles, I don't want to come off that way. I want it to be as a fellow musician and, more important, a musician they know of.

In that moment, I realize that things have to happen this way. I decide right then and there that I will make these men know the name Maceo Parker. I don't know how I'm going to do it, and I don't know how long it's going to take. But it's going to happen.

Then the words that will become a solemn promise to myself—the words that will forever shape the course of my life—come into my head and escape from my lips. I say them out loud, and although no one really hears, I know I mean every word.

"One of these days you're all gonna know me."

1

Teaching Little Fingers to Play

Oftentimes in interviews, reporters ask me for my earliest memory. To try to reach back that far in your mind is an interesting exercise (and I found myself doing it often as I wrote this book). If I close my eyes, my earliest memories are mostly of feelings—impressions, really. And the earliest and most indelible feeling is simply of love.

I was born Maceo Parker Junior on Valentine's Day, 1943, in a tiny row house at 121 Railroad Street in Kinston, North Carolina, just yards from the tracks that divided the black and white sections of the town. Perhaps my being born on the day that celebrates love was a good omen. Love and warmth filled our little house, a busy place with people constantly going in and out. I remember so many different faces. Two small ones soon became very familiar—that of my older brother, Kellis, who was born a year before me, and that of my younger brother, Melvin, who followed me in 1944. Before I knew the meaning of "brother," I felt a bond between us. It wasn't until I was around five, though, that I made the connection that we were more than just buddies. We were family.

My world consisted of our tiny house and the street that ran behind it, which was bordered by houses just like ours on either side. When my mother and father were around, I felt secure. My paternal grandmother, Eva, also lived with us for a time. Even my parents just called her Grandma. Throughout the day, she would call on my brothers and me to help her with little things, like adjusting her pillows or rubbing her feet. She died when I was very young.

We had a large family in Kinston, and holidays were always important times at our house. One of the earliest Christmases I can recall took place at that Railroad Street house when I was about four or five. I saw a picture of Santa Claus in an advertisement and discovered that he rode on a sleigh pulled by eight tiny reindeer. He was not, as I had previously believed, the nice old man who drove through the neighborhood at Christmastime and tossed candy from the window of his pickup truck. That Christmas morning, my brothers and I ran out to the tree like all little boys do, only to find there were no presents underneath. My mother explained that Santa Claus just "didn't come for some reason," but she said we still had a lot to be thankful for. I felt a little sad but tried not to show it. When we got to my grandparents' house that afternoon for supper, however, all of our presents were there waiting for us. My mother liked to play little practical jokes like that from time to time, a trait that would eventually rub off on my brother Melvin.

My brothers and I, being so close in age, were an especially tight-knit group. Like most young boys, we were proud of our gender and regarded girls, like our older cousin Eva Delores, as pests. Eva was named for Grandma and came to live with us for a time. She quickly became the Parker brothers' nemesis, partly because she was a girl, but mostly because she would tease us relentlessly.

Back then, my brothers and I shared a single bed, which we'd occasionally wet. We would clean ourselves really well, and honestly it was almost impossible to tell who had actually done the deed. Consequently, each of us would get a spanking for it the next morning. (My parents reasoned that this was the only way to be firm *and* fair.) For obvious reasons, Eva found this incredibly amusing and would laugh herself silly when it happened.

One day, Melvin had enough of her and talked Kellis and I into getting even. That afternoon, the three of us crept into her room, pulled the sheets back from her bed, and took turns peeing on her mattress. In the morning, she was the one getting a paddling, and we were the ones laughing. We still tease her about it to this day.

The occasional mischievous prank notwithstanding, my brothers and I were all well-behaved children. We were made to understand early on that it was important to behave ourselves; our mother repeated the phrase "Be good boys" like a mantra, reminding us that we were expected to conduct ourselves in a manner that wouldn't embarrass our family or our church. For me, misbehaving meant disrupting the warmth and love that filled the house, especially after my youngest brother, DeLond, was born in 1946.

In addition to the love and peace that existed in our home, music was there, too. It seemed like it was always in the air, whether someone was singing, listening to the radio, or playing records. My father, Maceo Parker Senior, played lots of Louis Jordan 78s in the evenings after supper. My mother, Novella, was always singing something in a rich gospel voice forged by years and years in the church choir, which my father participated in, too. Her voice would carry across the hardwood floors of the house to wherever I was and comfort me. If I could hear my mother singing, I knew everything was all right. If she wasn't singing, she was humming a happy tune, usually one I recognized from church.

From the beginning, I liked going to church, because I knew it wouldn't be too long before there would be lots of singing. It gave me my first real exposure to formal music. Saint Peter's Disciples Baptist Church was a small brick building less than a mile from our house. Sometimes my brothers and I would walk straight down the railroad tracks that ran in front of the house to get there. In between the tracks and the church was an empty lot, nicknamed the Stone Yard, that the city used for storing old concrete drainage pipes. They weren't quite large enough for an adult to walk through upright, but the older kids found them convenient when they needed a quiet place to be alone. We would cut through the Stone Yard as quickly as possible to avoid running into anyone there. Both parties were better off that way—the teenagers didn't want to be disturbed, and we didn't want to catch hell from them.

In the summers, my brothers and I would attend vacation bible school at Saint Peter's. If you brought your own Mason jar, you'd be greeted with a fresh glass of homemade lemonade to start the day. Sometimes in the afternoons, we'd each be given a nickel or two to buy a scoop of ice cream on the way home.

The church was like a second home with an extended family, and my mother and father were very well regarded there because they were so involved with the choir, something that made me very proud. They often hosted choir rehearsals at our house, which afforded me the opportunity to watch and listen to everything. We had an old upright piano in the corner of the house, and several times a week the choir would gather around it and practice the songs for that week's service. Even as a very young child, I would stop what I was doing and run over to that piano whenever someone started playing it.

One of my earliest and most vivid musical memories is of the piano itself. One afternoon, when I was about four years old, I strolled over to it and, barely tall enough to see over the keys, reached up and pushed down gently on one of the white ones. The sound it made was exhilarating, so I did it again, this time a little more forcefully. Entranced, I moved my hand left to right, pushing down on the keys, intrigued by the way the sound changed each time. A pattern started to take shape as I moved methodically up and down, key by key. After a while, I began to understand the relationship between the notes and the keys. If this was making music, I liked it. I was hooked.

From then on, whenever someone sat at that piano, I would be there, observing the relation of the pitch to where his fingers landed. Then, when no one was around, I'd climb up into the chair and try to emulate what I'd seen.

One afternoon, a gentleman from the church named Ronald Francis came to our house with the choir. Everyone gathered around him as he seated himself at the piano and started the introduction to a song they were working on. After he played a few bars, everyone began to sing:

> Yield not to temptation, for yielding is sin;
> Each victory will help you, some other to win;
> Fight manfully onward, dark passions subdue;
> Look ever to Jesus, He'll carry you through.

I watched Mr. Francis's fingers as they moved stepwise down with the melody and back up during each verse. The choir rehearsed the song several times, and when they were satisfied with it, they went into the kitchen to take a break. As soon as they were gone, I scrambled up into the piano chair and began to play what I'd just seen Mr. Francis play. At first, it came to me very slowly as I methodically tried to recall everything I'd seen, but soon the melody began to take shape with strong tones and steady rhythm. As I sang the melody softly to myself, my little fingers just fell in the right places. It all made sense.

The conversation in the kitchen quieted down, and it kept on quieting down until, eventually, no one was speaking. Then someone said, "That kid isn't playing that song, is he?"

One by one, the adults filed out and gathered around behind me, listening in disbelief until I finished the song. Everyone marveled at what I had done, and it gave me an enormous sense of accomplishment, especially when I saw my mother beaming with pride. From then on, she encouraged me to play the piano whenever I could. "Watch this child play the piano," she would say to a guest, and I would hoist myself up on the bench and oblige. I never missed an opportunity to play "Yield Not to Temptation" for someone. I liked making my mother smile.

Back then, my mother always seemed happy. Having some of that happiness directed right at me really motivated me to keep playing. By the time I was five years old, I found I could peck out a few more of the choir's regular spirituals just by observing how other people played. Music just came naturally to me. Some kids realize early on that they can throw the football really far or spell really well; I realized that I could hear melodies and play them back. And although I had many other interests, I began to feel how important music was. Once I opened that door, there was no shutting it again.

For my parents, music was a spiritual thing and an escape of sorts. Not until I was much older did I realize how hard they struggled back then. They were masters at creating a lighthearted atmosphere around the house, despite the cramped conditions and scarcity of money and food. Music helped hold everything together. It's difficult for me to imagine just how hard my parents worked to scratch out a living, but to them it was just a part of life. Coming of age in the 1930s the way they did—being two generations removed from slavery and living through the worst economic depression our country had ever seen—meant nothing came easy to them.

My father owned and operated the East End Dry Cleaners, the first black-owned dry-cleaning business in town. He had learned the trade during his time in the navy. The building where the cleaners was located is still standing today. It's at 407 Queen Street, not far from our house on Railroad Street (although now it's a barber shop). As a young man, my father served as an apprentice to the white owner of another dry-cleaning business in Kinston, but by his early twenties he had opened his own business with his younger brother, James.

My mother stayed at home primarily, but she found odd jobs cleaning or sewing to make a little extra money. She was a very resourceful woman. As a child, she used to gather small bouquets of wildflowers, bind them together with twine, and sell them on the streets of Kinston to make some money to bring home to her mother. She and her seven brothers and one sister would stand near the center of town and sing spirituals in beautiful four-part harmonies for spare change from passersby. Her family was very gifted musically.

In fact, music brought my parents together as teenagers. They attended an after-school music program together. My mother was the top female singer and my father was the top male singer, so they were often paired together for duets. They hit it off, became high school sweethearts, and were married shortly after their graduation. Now, I've never heard this exactly from my mother, but several people from her class have told me that she and my father were also incredible dancers in their day and won lots of dance contests at the summer street festivals in Kinston. (I've heard this more than once from different people, so I'm inclined to believe that it's true.) Somewhere along the way, though, their Saturday night dances tapered off, and their Sunday mornings in the church choir picked up.

In 1948, my parents moved our family from the ramshackle neighborhood on Railroad Street to the brand-new housing projects that had just been erected on Carver Court. Grandma had passed away by this time, but I think an uncle or cousin was staying with us. When we moved into our unit, 9D, we felt like we'd won the lottery. There was fresh paint on the walls and no cracks in the floorboards; it was a two-story mansion as far as I could tell.

In the corner of the property was a brand-new community center where my brothers and I would eventually hang out after school. We watched the older guys as they played music and danced, trying to impress girls. Mrs. Cox (who is in her eighties and still lives in Kinston) taught an arts and crafts class there that was really popular with the younger kids. The community center also organized little sports events, like a Pop Warner football league that Kellis played in. Our neighborhood would square off against other housing projects across town.

Back then, I wasn't aware of the term "low-income housing"; to me, it seemed like we had really come up in the world, and I was proud of where we lived. As kids, we felt a little superior because we went to the new "brick" school, J. H. Sampson Elementary, rather than to the old wooden one on the edge of town that had been around since my mother attended it. I recall the stigma around the kids who lived out in the rural areas. My group of friends seemed to look down on those whose addresses were tacked up on boxes on rural routes rather than on the fronts of houses on proper streets. I feel bad about it now, because I know those people had rough lives. Working in the cotton and tobacco fields was not easy, and I doubt that I would have ever had time for music had my family been tied to the land like that.

The old upright piano followed us to our new house, and so did choir practices. I still stood by the edge of the piano and watched whenever someone was playing and tried to cue in on what they were doing. I was five years old by this time, and I could play a few complete songs pretty well just by observing their actions.

Eventually someone mentioned piano lessons, and I became very excited. My parents somehow found the money and arranged lessons with the city librarian, Mrs. White. Every Tuesday, Thursday, and Friday after school, I'd walk the four blocks to her house for my 4:30 PM lesson. The book she taught from was called *Teaching Little Fingers to Play* because it was written for children whose small hands couldn't span very far on the piano; just about everything was within an octave's reach. The music may have been written for children, but that book was so big it looked like I was carrying a sandwich board under my arm. Compared to the church hymns I was used to hearing, the melodies to these beginning piano songs were fairly simple, and mostly I would just listen to what Mrs. White did and play that back from memory. I found it a little easier than trying to read and play at the same time.

Three times a week I would wait in Mrs. White's parlor with the other students until my name was called. It wasn't long before I began to notice that all of her other students were girls. Every afternoon I would wait for another boy student to appear—I had seen plenty of men at the piano at my house—but none came. This troubled me a bit. I was used to being with my brothers all the time and was suspicious of anything that little girls were into. I worried that the other boys in my first-grade class would label me a sissy if they found out where I was going three times a week. I began to seriously consider quitting. Music was important, but it wasn't the only thing that I could do well. I found that I ran faster than anyone in my class, and in elementary school the fastest kid in the class is something of a celebrity. And I was popular. After a few months, I decided it just wasn't worth risking that for piano lessons. Besides, learning the piano came so naturally that I figured I could just continue learning by watching. My parents were supportive of my decision and told me that, if that's what I wanted to do, they wouldn't make me go.

I then had more time to help out with the family. When my brothers and I were needed, we'd go help my father and my uncle James down at the cleaners. They would give us several giant boxes of hangers, and our job was to attach a folded piece of cardboard, called a pants guard, to the bottom of each one. (It kept your trousers from getting a nasty crease from the wire.) Our day's work was long and tedious, but it was nothing compared to what my father and uncle had to do to keep that place going. To heat up enough water to create the steam needed, they had to constantly shovel coal into this giant furnace. My father had to pull open the furnace door with a shovel each time because it was too hot to touch.

It was sweaty, backbreaking work, but I wished I was old enough to be given that job. I wanted to do something more important than just assembling hangers. I wanted to get my hands dirty.

I would get my wish occasionally when the coal man came through the alley behind Queen Street and deposited a giant load for my father. My brothers and I had the job of filling the buckets and bringing them inside. That work felt important, and it was a lot more fun than messing around with hangers all afternoon. Every once in a while, one of us would pick up a stray piece of coal and send it whizzing through the air—right into the back of someone else's head. We were little boys, and horsing around just came with the territory. Even when we were hard at work, we were still little boys at heart.

My father didn't tolerate much horseplay at the cleaners, though. The back room was filled with all kinds of machinery and chemicals, and we weren't allowed in there. All the cleaned garments were bagged and alphabetized on a long rack in the back. Some of the clear bags had become dusty and translucent with age because the people who'd dropped off their cleaning hadn't come back to pick it up. My father still hung on to these old clothes, sometimes for years, waiting for people to come back and claim them. Clothes seemed to be piled up *everywhere*. It was pretty dark in the back, so you had to know where the paths through all the mounds of clothes were.

Tripping over clothes wasn't the only hazard. All of the machinery in the back—the industrial-sized washers, dryers, and pressing tables—had the potential to severely injure someone. A machine called the tumbler took the clothes from the washer and spun all the excess water out of them before they went into the dryer. We kids called it "the fumbler."

One afternoon, Uncle James was there cleaning some of his clothes. He tried to pull one of his shirts from the fumbler while it was still spinning. When he reached in to grab it, his arm became entangled in the wet laundry, and the machine spun him around violently, smashing his head into a support beam. He was killed instantly.

His funeral was held several days later, and it was an awful experience. Everyone wore black that day, even the choir. The songs they sang weren't the hand-clapping hymns I was used to. They were somber and heavy and interrupted by the sounds of

cookie from each plate before the rest of us got there. He was a practical joker even then.

I was still playing the piano. My mother could see how drawn I was to music, so she would take us out to see the local marching bands whenever she could. One year, my mother took us to watch Kinston's annual Christmas parade. I was completely drawn to the spectacle of the marching band. Before I even understood the concept of fanfare, I loved the way the sound of a horn section grew and expanded—it breathed like the choir music of church but had the piercing sound of the brass. I had heard plenty of big-band music, but there was something thrilling about the marching band—the starched uniforms with epaulettes, the precise movements, the cheering of the crowd. I knew right then that I wanted to play *that* music.

When my mother explained that the marching band had no pianos, I was disappointed, but only for a little while. I decided that I would just have to learn a new instrument. When a row of saxophone players marched by, stepping in unison and pivoting their horns side to side with real precision, I told my mother, "I want to learn to play one of those."

That one spontaneous decision would shape the rest of my life in a way that almost no other decision has. My mother agreed to look into renting one for me, and I happily went back to watching the parade. That Monday, I walked into my class and proudly announced to my teacher that I was going to be a saxophone player when I grew up.

By this time, Kellis was already playing trombone, and Melvin was picking up the drums from my uncle Bobby. Bobby's band, the Blue Notes, played all the jazz standards, ballads, and a bunch of popular R&B tunes of the day. They were a popular local group that worked steadily in area nightclubs. In addition to hosting church-choir practices, our house also served as an informal rehearsal space for the group. We boys would sit around while they practiced their set, soaking it all up. After hearing some of the same songs week after week, my brothers and I began to practice songs from their routine, like "Heavy Juice" and "Blue Moon." I really got into one tune, called "Intermission Riff," because I loved the way the melody climbed up in half-step intervals. It taught me to transpose a melody into many different keys. We eventually got it down and practiced it all the time.

Bobby was fond of a ballad called "Gratefully." Ask any jazz musician: playing a ballad is not as easy as it sounds. Just because the tempo is slow and the chords don't come at you fast, people naturally assume it is much easier to play. But it's all about your phrasing, or the way you're able to weave a melody out of both long, sustained notes and shorter ones. Back then, I was really drawn to guys like King Curtis who played a lot of staccato phrases. I tried to apply that approach to playing ballads but had very little success.

I decided to do some research. I realized I really liked the way trumpet players like Lee Morgan, Freddie Hubbard, and Clifford Brown played ballads, especially the way they'd hold a note until just the right moment. When they played the melody, they'd almost never play it straight; they'd color it with little flourishes here and there, connecting the long notes with short, fast phrases. I started emulating these cats and almost immediately found that my ballad playing improved. Melvin still jokes about the way I used to play "Gratefully," though.

Our cousin Timothy was a trumpet player and lived in the same housing projects; he started practicing with the three of us regularly. The four of us were obsessed with music, soaking up as much from as many different places as we could. We wanted to listen to *everything*. Timothy's father, my uncle Frank, also loved music; he would have us over some nights to watch Jimmy and Tommy Dorsey or Lawrence Welk on his television set, which was a real treat for us because we didn't own one. Televisions were something of a luxury on Carver Court back in those days.

An older boy named Joe Nobles, whose family had also moved to Carver Court from the old Railroad Street neighborhood, had a pretty healthy record collection and would let us come by to hear something new he'd just picked up. We would listen to a record over and over again and then try to play it by ear. The years of piano paid off—I was pretty fast at figuring out the melodies, which meant I could help Kellis and Timothy figure out their parts. Even back then, we were figuring out arrangements for jazz tunes just like a big band would do. This type of arranging was pretty sophisticated for three elementary school kids who were playing by ear; it also meant our arrangements were really unique.

Now, when I say we played all the time, I mean we played *all the time*. Our next-door neighbor, a gentleman by the name of Mr. Brown, had several small children at home. He used to tell my mother that when his kids got old enough, he was going to buy them instruments so they could repay us for all the "entertainment" we'd given him. Mr. Brown was joking, but it must have been difficult to deal with at first. We were constantly playing music, and I'm sure it didn't sound that great in the beginning.

After a few months of rehearsing, though, we started to get some positive feedback from our parents and the guys in our uncle's band. This encouragement was all we needed, and one afternoon we decided to form a real band. We named ourselves the Junior Blue Notes after Bobby's band. We got even more serious about music and practiced twice as much and twice as hard as before. Uncle Bobby was so impressed with our progress after several months that, after talking it over with my mother and Uncle Frank, he offered us a spot at his band's next performance. When the band took their break, we would have the chance to get up onstage and keep things going. We knew only three or four songs all the way through, but that didn't matter. The Junior Blue Notes had a gig!

We worked extra hard that week, and on Friday evening Bobby came around to drive us to the gig. We were deposited in the band's dressing room. While they played their first set, we listened through the walls, too excited to sit still. We could hear people laughing and talking, but when the band would finish a song, the crowd always responded with a big round of applause. I wondered if they were going to clap like that for our band.

When the Blue Notes were ready for a break, we were brought out and introduced as the Junior Blue Notes. I wasn't really sure what to expect, but I had an enormous amount of confidence in our band. That feeling had a lot to do with our family's constant encouragement. We weren't really nervous about performing—we were anxious to see how people would respond.

As we kicked off our first tune, the audience watched us with mild interest, probably expecting us to be barely tolerable, if not downright terrible. But, by the end of our first song, I noticed people were genuinely smiling and clapping, surprised that a group of kids could play like that. We were actually *good*.

The rest of the set was a blur. Afterward we were promptly escorted back to the safety of the dressing room—but not before we'd had a chance to bask in the glow of the applause we'd earned.

That night, for the first time, I felt the sensation of entertaining complete strangers. I knew right away that it wasn't like playing for your family; something was different about the way those people cheered us on. Your family will support you no matter what you sound like, but an audience of strangers doesn't owe you any kind of sympathy. I realized if we could get them to clap and cheer us on the way they did after our first gig, we must really be on to something. It was a powerful feeling, and I wanted more.

We still didn't have a full repertoire, but we started making appearances at the local hot spots around town and asking to sit in with whatever band was performing that night. Most times, the bands were accommodating, even encouraging, and before long we were semiregular fixtures at the nightclubs in Kinston.

One particular band tried to show us up by learning a song we liked to play in a different key. Most tenor players are comfortable with the key of B flat, but ask them to play the same song up a half step, in the key of B natural, and everything comes apart. I tried to adjust to the new fingering, but without practicing in that key, it was nearly impossible. Their little joke made us look really bad in front of the audience that night, but it taught me a valuable lesson: learn to play in all twelve keys.

We recovered from that incident, and in no time we were accompanying the Blue Notes to all their gigs. We played our best songs while they took a breather during the intermissions. Within a few months, we added other tunes, like "Blue Moon" and "Gratefully," to our repertoire and had enough music to fill a full set.

Eventually the time came for us to look for our own gig. One of our first was for a PTA function. We had to audition for the association's members after one of their meetings, but since my mother and Tim's father, my uncle Frank, were both on the board, we felt like we had a pretty good shot.

The plan was to play a popular tune called "Cherry Pink (and Apple Blossom White)." It was a hit song for Pérez Prado, the same guy who wrote "Mambo Number 5" in 1955. The song has a Latin feel to it, but we decided we would put our own stamp on it. The way we worked it out, Melvin would start the tune off with a really funky drum vamp for a few measures before hitting his crash cymbal to kick off the song. On cue, Tim would begin the song's famous four-note opening riff and, with a nod of his head, conduct Kellis and me into the rest of the melody. We rehearsed for weeks because we really wanted to impress all the parents, and we nailed it every time. We were excited and pleased with ourselves because we knew we were really going to kill during the audition—they'd hire us for sure.

The day of the audition, Melvin somehow forgot the tiny wing nut that locks the crash cymbal down onto the stand. We didn't think it was a big deal, so no one really worried about it.

That afternoon, while the meeting went on, we set up behind the curtain in the auditorium. When it was finished, someone came to the stage to introduce our band to the crowd of parents and faculty. The stage curtain was old and rickety and only opened in small increments; each pull on the rope produced a creaking noise and only drew the curtain open another few inches. When the curtain was finally pulled back, we were given the nod to start. Melvin launched right into his drum vamp as planned, funky as ever. But when he hit the crash to start the tune, all hell broke loose. Instead of the tight *crash* sound we were expecting, the cymbal catapulted off the stand and hit the floor on its side with a very nonmusical *bing* that rang out through the entire auditorium.

The three of us up front, our horns to our lips, just stood there and watched out of the corners of our eyes as the cymbal rolled up to the front of the stage. The whole way down, it made this sort of *wah-wah* sound that got progressively louder until it hit the end of the stage, tipped over, and began to gyrate wildly on its edge. The *wah-wah* got louder and louder as it wobbled faster and faster— *wah wah wah WAH WAH WAH*—until it just stopped abruptly with a *SHHHTT!*

All the adults in the audience, including my mother, had their hands over their mouths, trying to stifle their laughter and spare our feelings. The band just waited nervously for Timothy to start the tune. For a moment, he looked as if he were going to, as if nothing out of the ordinary had happened. He took a deep breath and started to blow, but instead of playing the first note, he just cracked up laughing, right into his mouth piece.

That was it. The band started laughing, and all the parents started laughing out loud. I don't think we even played the song for them that afternoon. We still got the gig, probably out of pity, and played their PTA function, this time with the cymbal tightened down extra hard.

It was a rough beginning, but I knew I was on to something with the band—we all were. Melvin was very influenced by my uncle's drumming but was also beginning to incorporate different elements from some of the drummers we heard on the recordings we loved. Kellis was always very disciplined and studious, something we teased him about all the time, but dedication made him a technically solid trombone player. I had begun to isolate elements and phrases from different horn players that I liked and was incorporating those ideas into my playing. I found myself coming closest to Hank Crawford's style (although he played alto and I was playing tenor at the time). I felt like I understood his approach to playing a solo, especially when it came to ballads. David "Fathead" Newman was a close second. He had this way of wrapping his phrases around what the band was doing. He could take any idea he had and make it fit right in with the texture; he had this boldness in his sound that I wanted. But I never wanted to outright copy Hank or Fathead or anyone else. My skin used to crawl when someone would say I sounded "just like" King Curtis or Boots Randolph. Their playing influenced me, sure, but I always made it a point to modify what I was learning and bend it to fit my own concept. For instance, whereas Hank Crawford might lay into some really long tones, I would break them up into shorter rhythmic phrases that gave the solo some bounce, made it funkier. Same notes, different concept. I was searching for something.

I was also searching for acceptance by other musicians. When older cats like my uncle took an interest in what we were doing, it felt like we belonged to this special fraternity where people recognized us as musicians and, even better, wanted us to sit in and be a part of what they were doing.

Not everyone was ready to welcome us into this fraternity, though. My brothers and I were walking to the swimming pool one afternoon and heard some guys rehearsing in a garage. We thought they were pretty good, so we stopped to listen. They immediately stopped playing and told us that it was a "closed session." We weren't welcome even to sit there. Being rejected like that was a slap in the face, but fortunately this behavior wasn't common. More often than not, other musicians were very supportive.

One night, I recall looking up at the stars on my way home and imagining all the twinkling lights as saxophone players in the world, each one completely unique. I pictured my star squeezing in between some of the stars that were my influences. I figured if these stars, these players, could work at developing their own sound, then I could too. There were lots of bright lights up there, but I realized there was plenty of room for one more. Suddenly finding my own voice on the saxophone didn't seem like such a far-fetched idea anymore. I could hear someone on the jukebox and know who it was instantly, and I wanted people to hear my playing and say, "I *know* that's Maceo Parker."

Very soon, I would be introduced to the man who would show me exactly how to make that happen.

2

I Remember Mr. Banks

I can't help but feel nostalgic for my childhood in Kinston. If my brothers and I weren't rehearsing for a Junior Blue Notes gig, we were jumping into a pickup game of basketball or touch football with the other kids of the Carver Court projects or attending Boy Scout meetings. My friends and I were always clowning around, especially when we were supposed to be serious. During the recitation of the Boy Scout motto, we'd alter the credo a bit: *On my honor I will do my best to take what they give me and steal the rest!* We thought that was hilarious, although our scout leaders didn't find it nearly as funny. Of course we would never steal anything; our mother's mantra, "Be good boys," was firmly ingrained by then, and my brothers and I were well mannered most of the time.

Cutting up was just part of my personality, though. In school, I was the class clown. Before I ever became serious about music, I was already used to performing, because that's essentially what a class clown does. I would get giggles from some of the little girls, which gave me some satisfaction. I knew what was funny and what was disrespectful, though, so most of the time my teachers took it all in stride.

Some did not, however. One of my seventh-grade teachers, Mrs. Sarah Mae Hill, overheard me telling someone that I didn't study for her class. She punished me by swatting me across my knuckles with a ruler one afternoon. I was terribly confused.

"Why are you punishing me?" I asked her. I was making an A in her class and obviously didn't need to study.

"When I tell you to study, that means I want you to study," she replied.

Schoolwork seemed to come pretty easy to me without much studying, and, despite Mrs. Hill's intervention, I didn't see the benefit in doing so until much later.

Overall, I really enjoyed school. Some of my friends grumbled about having to go to class all of the time, especially when we left elementary school for junior high, but to me it was almost all fun in one way or another. I was not only in the school band, but I was also still one of fastest boys in the entire school, something I continued to take an enormous amount of pride in. I was never much of a basketball or baseball star. But when I went out for the football team later on, my speed really set me apart.

I wasn't completely serious about becoming a great musician yet. Like most kids my age, I had a wide range of interests, and music—though very important—was just one of many things that occupied my time. It wasn't until I was nearly in high school that my outlook on music changed entirely.

James Banks blew into Kinston like a cool breeze. In 1956, midway through my eighth-grade year, he became the new junior high and high school band director. A tall, broad-shouldered man, impeccably dressed and well-groomed, Mr. Banks wasn't like any teacher at that school—or anyone in town, for that matter. He had traveled around the world as a warrant officer in the army and carried himself with the kind of sophisticated swagger that attracted attention. His charisma and charm made him instantly popular with the faculty and students alike. All the drum majorettes at school (and quite a few of the female teachers) were wild about him, despite the fact that he had a beautiful young wife who taught at the elementary school. Even his car, a shiny Mercury he called "Big M," was an extension of his outgoing persona. Mr. Banks—or "Banks," as he eventually became known to me—was just *cool.*

On his first day leading our eighth-grade band, Banks introduced himself to the class. Then he casually began leafing through our book of sheet music until he found a piece near the back that he liked. Without practicing or rehearsing any of it, he had the entire band play the piece from sight.

This task was, as you can imagine, nearly impossible for an eighth-grade band. After a few measures, the entire thing began to fall apart. Banks just smiled and had the band continue reading through the piece, all the way to the end, even though we sounded more like a traffic jam than a marching band.

After we finished, everyone looked around at each other, a bit bewildered. Smiling, Banks just flipped through the music book to another composition and had the band sight-read that one as well. No one really knew what to make of this man, but it was obvious that he was a very unorthodox band leader. I liked him instantly.

This sight-reading exercise appeared to be organized chaos, but Banks was actually gauging everyone's skill level. In no time at all, he had rearranged the band the way he saw fit, identifying the more skilled players and separating them from those who needed some work. Another eighth-grade student and I were singled out and assigned to a more advanced band, which was composed mostly of high school students.

One day, after a rehearsal, Banks approached me while I was packing up my horn.

"Maceo," he said, "I want you to come back here to the band hall during your lunch period today."

I wasn't sure exactly what he wanted, but I was curious. When lunch rolled around, I ate in a hurry and ran over with my saxophone as fast as I could.

As I walked in, I heard him really play for the first time—and was completely stunned. I had liked Banks's personality from the start, but it wasn't until I heard the man play, and I mean really *play*, that he truly inspired me. He had this incredibly polished sound that I had only heard on recordings. It was wide and expansive like Fathead Newman's and as dynamic as Hank Crawford's or Sonny Stitt's. Banks did not sound like a student, or even a teacher. He sounded like a professional.

I stood there in the doorway of the band hall and just listened to him for a while, mesmerized. I made up my mind right then and there to learn whatever I could from this man. I wanted to sound just like he did—not to play exactly like him, but to have a sound that was as polished and refined as his. I wanted to sound like a professional too.

For the better part of the next four years, I ate my lunch in the hallways of the high school and spent my lunch periods in the band hall working on my sound with Banks. He would run everyone out of the room when I got there, and the two of us would just play.

In the beginning, he started off by playing a short phrase and asking me to repeat it back. He said to me, "Now, you keep playing that phrase over and over until, when you play it after me, it's impossible for anyone to tell the difference."

We did this exercise day after day for months on end. The point of it was to focus my attention on my tone and really craft the notes. For months, we hardly did anything else in our private tutoring sessions.

By the time I was well into in high school, my sound had greatly matured, and Banks started giving me important solos during our concerts. Once he gave me the solo in the middle of a Lionel Hampton tune, but he scripted out the first four measures of it for me.

"You can play whatever you want afterward," he said, "but I want you to start it out with these four measures."

By this time, our relationship had developed into a real mentoring friendship, and I felt comfortable questioning his methods occasionally.

"Why do I have to start my solo like that?" I asked him.

He shot me a blank stare and with a slight grin told me to "just do it." Mine was a friendly protest but one he put to rest immediately.

Other times, though, my defiance was a little more blatant. In my sophomore year of high school, the band was short several flute players for our Christmas concert. Without asking for volunteers, Banks simply conscripted several of the saxophone players into the flute section, including me. I was really angry about it because I had no interest in playing the flute. "I don't play flute," I told him, "and that's all there is to it." Looking back, I think he asked me to do it because he knew he could count on me, but at the time I took it as a slight. Banks wasn't happy about my insurrection, but I think he let it slide because I was his protégé.

During my high school years, our mentoring relationship extended beyond the classroom. When I turned sixteen in February 1959, I took my driver's license test and passed it; I told Banks about it immediately. He seemed really proud of me, and from then on he started having me run errands in his car, Big M.

I picked up supplies or drove his wife home in the afternoons. On the weekends, when Banks wasn't playing his horn, he was tinkering around under the hood of his beloved car, and I would stop by his house and talk to him while he worked on the engine. He knew about my gigs with the Junior Blue Notes and was always very curious about how they were going. I invited him to attend important performances of mine, and he showed up fairly often to watch me play. It was a big honor to have him in the audience, and I played extra well when he was there. Occasionally he would bring his horn and sit in with our band, which gave me an indescribable mixture of pride, elation, and anxiety. (I felt this way again many years later, when I was called on to share the stage with one of my greatest musical influences, Ray Charles.) Because my father was gone so often during this time, Banks became a role model for me, someone I tried to emulate in many ways, especially musically.

By this time, the Junior Blue Notes—now called the Mighty Blue Notes—had become one of the premier bands in the Kinston area and regularly gigged two to three nights every weekend. A young man named Ulysses Hardy became our piano player and band manager. He had returned to Kinston after a stint in the air force and lived on East Street, a popular strip where some of the local clubs were located. (Years later I composed a tune for my album *Roots Revisited* called "Up and Down East Street" as an homage to it.) Since Ulysses was a bit older than we were, he had more leverage when it came to dealing with club owners; for that reason, he managed the band and handled our finances.

Like a lot of all-black bands in those days, we played both black and white establishments without much thought to the politics of it. Harlem's Inn on East Street was an upscale spot where you could get a nice dinner and listen to a band on the weekends;

it was especially popular with the date crowd. A guy who was looking to impress a young lady would reserve a nice table there and listen to the Mighty Blue Notes all night. Some of the other clubs on East Street were a bit rougher, like the One Ten or Wooten's Alley. As kids, we watched Saturday matinees featuring John Wayne, Lash LaRue, and Roy Rogers at the Arcadian Lounge, but by the time we were in high school, we were playing gigs there on Friday and Saturday nights to a much different crowd.

Ulysses made a great addition to the band not only because he was a good piano player and manager but also because he had a car, which considerably extended our range for playing gigs. When we didn't have gigs in and around Kinston, our band was on the road, playing gigs all over eastern North Carolina. We became especially popular in the town of Faison, where a man by the name of Ellis, who owned a pickle company, converted his pickle warehouse into a dance hall on the weekends. He put sawdust out on the floor and set out snacks and drinks next to a makeshift stage. Soon he was advertising the concerts with fliers tacked up all around town. We became the house favorites of the white college kids, who would come from as far away as Virginia. These gigs were always fun for us. Although we were playing to mostly white audiences who absolutely loved us, we didn't socialize much when the gigs were over. We generally finished our last song, loaded the car, and headed back to Kinston.

One night after the show, a young man approached the band with an interesting offer.

"Do you guys have to be home by a certain time?" he asked us.

My brothers and I didn't have a curfew, so we told him we were in no rush.

"How would you guys feel about coming back to my house and playing there for me and my friends?" he asked.

Nobody really spoke up because we were all thinking the same thing. We didn't know this guy and weren't convinced going out to his house was a good idea. Still, he wasn't drunk and seemed nice enough, so we entertained the idea.

After a few minutes of listening to us talk indecisively amongst ourselves, the guy blurted out, "I'll give you five dollars a minute."

That phrase stopped everyone cold.

"Are you serious?" I asked.

The young man assured me he was, so I did some quick math in my head and figured out that he was talking about three hundred dollars an hour. That was some serious money.

After a quick consultation with Ulysses, the band agreed to drive out to this guy's place and play for a while. We loaded the car and followed him out to a house in a remote neighborhood well outside of town. We knew we were taking a chance by agreeing to do this, but the money he was offering was too good to pass up.

When we finally arrived at the house, the guy went around gathering up the people who were milling about and waking up those who had already gone to bed. Quite a few people were there, as it turned out. We set up and played our set right there in this guy's living room. The people danced and partied all around us, some still in their pajamas.

It wasn't long, though, before we heard a couple of gunshots down the road. Then, a few seconds later, we heard more shots— only this time they were louder. Whoever was out there was getting closer to the house. They were obviously not happy about the late-night partying and were on their way over to voice their displeasure.

As much fun as we were having, the band realized it was time for us to call it a night and head home, so we began to break down and load up the car. To this day, I joke with Melvin about how fast he put his drums away. Normally he would take his time packing things up, but Melvin beat *everyone* into the car that night.

As we started to pull out of the driveway, the welcome wagon arrived and surrounded the car. We were confronted by a group of local "good old boys." They were less than happy to see four young black men in their neighborhood, especially at three in the morning. They demanded to know what we were doing there, and without shutting off the engine or leaving the car, we politely explained that we were a band who was invited out to play the house party. We assured them that we were on our way out, and they agreed that it was in our best interests to leave town immediately. Luckily we made it out of there with the three hundred dollars from the house party that night, although no amount of money could have lured us out there again.

From then on, whenever we had a gig in Faison, we would drive out of town right after the gig on the little tobacco road that led back to Kinston. And each time as we drove home, waiting at the edge of town in the glow of our headlights, was the same group of good old boys there to make sure we weren't about to do any more late-night entertaining in their neck of the woods.

Most of the time, though, our gigs went off without a hitch, no matter what our audience looked like. We had played to different audiences since we were kids, and because we acted like professionals, we were—for the most part—treated as such.

Segregation was an ugly, undeniable fact that I just learned to deal with. That isn't to say that I ignored or blindly accepted it. Living with segregation meant you acknowledged it but structured your life to afford you the most dignity. Living this way usually meant avoiding situations where your pride could be compromised. For instance, I could accept the fact that the black movie theater in town would get the newly released pictures weeks and weeks after the white theater had shown them. That was just how it was. What I would *not* do, however, was go to the white theater, enter through the back door, and sit quietly in the balcony. I preferred instead to wait until the film came to the black theater, when I could enter through the front door and sit wherever I pleased. Similarly, if a restaurant in town only served its black patrons out of a window by the back door, I didn't eat there. I chose to preserve my dignity by not playing *that* game.

The game went both ways, though, because playing gigs was another matter entirely. My brothers and I played at both segregated clubs and venues with all-white audiences regularly while we were in high school. We would not turn down money for a gig, regardless of what color our audience was or how the establishment operated. It was just too important to our family to keep a steady income rolling in. If the three of us could work three nights a week gigging, we would have a lot of money come Monday morning. Making money was more important than making a statement.

This kind of compromise always bothered Kellis the most. When I was a junior in high school, he was a senior, and he had been elected student-body president. One of the first things he did was organize an antisegregation march. He was very official about the entire thing, from organizing the students to notifying the Kinston police of his intent to peacefully demonstrate downtown. By that time, the civil rights movement had splintered in several directions. I was always a fan of Dr. Martin Luther King Jr.'s nonviolent approach; I agreed that two wrongs didn't make a right. Kellis really believed in this philosophy as well, something that is easy to preach but difficult to do. To successfully demonstrate the way King was able to, a nonviolent "game plan" had to be well in place beforehand, because there were sure to be people who didn't appreciate what you were doing and who would try to provoke you.

Kellis was superb at organizing and preparing everyone for what to expect. His efforts were impressive, and I was proud to get behind them—literally. At the demonstration, they stuck me in the back because my voice was loud. With our songs, slogans, and signs, we made a statement that we, the black population, were an equal part of the community, deserving of equal rights under the law—and it was time *everyone* recognized that.

Kellis's demonstration was a huge success, and as a result several establishments in Kinston—including the theater and several drugstore lunch counters—eventually desegregated. This victory foreshadowed the direction Kellis's life would take. The following year, 1960, he, along with three other young black students, would be admitted to the University of North Carolina—the first people to integrate that campus.

I think a major reason for the march's success was that there wasn't any hatred in our message. We all acknowledged the way things were "once upon a time," back in our grandfathers' day. But there had been a steady culture of integration and change since then, and we simply wanted everyone to acknowledge that this evolution must continue. The way we saw it, that was then and this was now. We were committed to doing whatever needed to be done to bring about change.

Every year, our high school's marching band performed at Kinston's Christmas parade along with the band from the local white high school. It stung a bit that we were forced to march in the back of the parade, despite the fact that, year after year, we were the better band. Again, that was just how things were, and we begrudgingly accepted it. Melvin never really liked this arrangement, though. Playing the drums for several hours was extremely physically demanding. Most drummers would take a break and rest their arms at some point during the performance, and as long as not all of them rested at the same time, everything was cool. One year, Melvin told me that he was going to play the entire parade without stopping. I thought he was crazy, but he surprised everyone and did it. He paid for it afterward with sore shoulders and blistered hands, but he could be stubbornly determined like that. It was his way of making a statement.

In the summer of 1959, "What'd I Say" was released in two parts and was a huge hit for Ray Charles. I heard John R., a popular AM radio disc jockey out of Nashville, play this song one night, and I was *hooked*. I got a copy of that record soon after. I would sprint home from school in the afternoons and listen to it over and over again while my brothers and I cleaned the house. Melvin and I jumped around singing the call-and-response parts at the top of our lungs. I was already a big fan of Ray and his band, but this record represented a new level of appreciation for me. We tore up the house we were so excited.

I was fortunate enough to see Ray that same year, when he came to Kinston to play a concert at an old tobacco warehouse. Just about everyone I knew went, but for me it was more than a concert. It was a pilgrimage.

When I arrived, I could hear the music well enough but wasn't able to see the stage from the back, so I had to push my way through the crowd. I was determined to *see* this man and his band, not just to hear them. As I jostled through a sea of shoulders and elbows, I suddenly found myself up against a large white rope, the nautical kind used to moor ships to the dock. It had been strung from one end of the stage to the back of the warehouse. One look on the other side of the rope told me all I needed to know about its purpose: white folks on one side, black folks on the other.

Everyone in that warehouse that night, white and black alike, bumped along to "Hit the Road, Jack" and "I Got a Woman," singing and clapping like they were in church. We were just one massive soul congregation all moving together. I stood there beside that gigantic rope the entire night, dancing next to people I was technically forbidden to socialize with. As much as I enjoyed that show, the message of that rope left a bad taste in my mouth. (I'm happy to say that, the next time I saw Ray in Kinston, it wasn't there.)

I mention this night because the experience has really shaped the message I give in my music today—a message of love. I want people to listen to my music and forget about what happened at work that day, forget about the bills they need to pay, forget about all the war and suffering in the world, and just dance. When an audience arrives for a Maceo Parker show, I feel it's my mission to do what Ray Charles's music did for the audience that night: I want to make *everyone* feel uplifted by love.

Melvin and I were going to see a lot of performers, including Chuck Berry and James Brown, in the area. I knew most of the songs from the radio, but seeing them performed live was something else entirely. After the shows, Melvin and I would talk about every exciting little detail we noticed. It seemed like the more shows we went to, the more we realized that we could do what these performers were doing. By this time, we had been playing so long that we had developed a real confidence in our abilities. That's not to say that we thought we were as good as or better than James Brown, for instance—we just understood that James's music was essentially very simple, and what set him apart was his performance of that music. We were still in awe of the performance, but we felt like we could not only play the music, but we could play it just as well. More and more, making a career out of music began to seem like a seriously attainable goal.

It was already working out financially. With the money Kellis, Melvin, and I were making every weekend gigging, coupled with my mother's income and what my father was able to send home, our family was actually doing well. We were able to move out of the Carver Court projects and into a new house at 703 Liberty Hill Road, which was was much larger than our cramped apartment and was in a much nicer black neighborhood. Occasionally, when I'm feeling nostalgic, I will take a drive over to this house. In the front yard is a large tree that my family planted shortly after we moved in there in 1958. I can still remember how proud my brothers and I were when we moved in. It was certainly a step up for my family, and our dedication to music was partially responsible.

The move meant I lived much closer to a girl named Velma Dove, who I had been dating for some time. Velma's father, Milton, owned a successful automotive business in Kinston, and she and her family lived in an impressive house several blocks away from our new house. They were wealthy by our standards, and although I was proud of our move out of the projects, I always got a little nervous when she decided to make the walk down the hill and ring my doorbell. I was more comfortable going to her house, which, by comparison, was palatial.

Velma was very pretty, incredibly smart, and as serious about school as I was about music. We still managed to find time to do all of the things usual high school sweethearts do. We went to movies and concerts together and hung out after school. And, like most kids our age, we found ourselves curious about that most taboo of subjects: sex. I can honestly tell you that Velma and I were good kids in this respect; whenever we occasionally found ourselves in a compromising situation, one or both of us had the sense to put the brakes on before things went too far. By the time we graduated high school, we knew of some people who'd let their passions get the better of them and had to set aside their dreams because of it. She and I were both too committed to going to college to let that happen to us.

High school was a time of great self-discovery, and by my junior year I decided that I needed to continue expanding my horizons and try something new. Since our high school didn't have a track team, football seemed like the next obvious choice. It was never a passion of mine the way that music was, and not having ever played on a team before put me at a real disadvantage when I decided to join. At the time, I thought I was just a terrible athlete, but I think my biggest problem was inexperience. I worked hard during practice to learn the plays and minimize mistakes, and although I made the team, I never saw much playing time on the field. My football stint didn't stop me from playing music, though. I still belonged to the marching band, and during halftime I would march in my football uniform.

By my senior year, Banks had left his position as band director and taken a job touring with Lloyd Price. I was sad to see him leave, but I was more proud that my mentor was out on the road with a top-notch band. I entertained ideas of doing something similar, but becoming a full-time musician seemed like a big risk. I had made the decision to go to college, and getting a degree in music seemed like a good compromise. I figured after college I would get a job directing a high school band and mentoring young musicians the way Banks had mentored me. As incredibly tempting as going out on the road was, it seemed like an unrealistic goal.

Something I had overheard years before stuck in my head when I thought about being a full-time musician. Chuck Berry had been performing at Kinston's tobacco warehouse, and one evening I walked by a group of women talking to each other on their porch about the upcoming show.

"Are you going to that Chuck Berry concert?" one asked.

"No," her friend replied. "You know those musicians only care about drinking and taking drugs. I don't want any part of that."

I was shocked. I played in nightclubs just about every weekend, and I wasn't into drugs and alcohol. I knew that Banks, a man I greatly admired, wasn't that type of performer either. My brothers and I were young aspiring musicians, and we felt a sense of camaraderie and fellowship with other musicians. What that woman said sounded like an insult to everyone in my profession. It bounced around in my head for years, and it really bothered me. It was the first time I realized that such a negative stigma was attached to the word "musician," and I decided to change that if I ever became a professional.

As it turned out, that was only a few short years away. But, after I graduated high school, I was focused on starting my first semester at the university I'd chosen: North Carolina Agricultural and Technical State University.

3

Be Good Boys

I arrived at A&T as a freshman in the music program in the fall of 1961. The beautiful campus is in Greensboro, in the state's Piedmont region, just east of the Appalachian Mountains. This location put me in easy reach of all the state's major cities, an ideal place for a young musician to be if he was willing to travel a little. Since I was already used to playing out-of-town gigs and getting in late, I wasn't worried too much about how this schedule would affect school (although I should have been).

I was under the impression that the purpose of college was to get a degree that would eventually land me a teaching job somewhere. For me, studying music was going to be my ticket to becoming a band director at a high school or junior high, probably somewhere in North Carolina, and I figured I'd spend my days teaching kids marching routines for halftime shows. During those first few weeks on campus that fall, I spent my time hard at work in this pursuit, learning my music for the football games, going to class, and studying.

Still, I couldn't stop thinking of Banks and how incredible it was that he was out on the road with Lloyd Price. His departure had planted a seed in my mind that had grown into a serious desire to be a touring musician. I was as terrified of being stuck in the same place for the rest of my life as some people are afraid to get on a plane or board a ship. I could see myself in a rocking chair on my front porch many, many years into the future, wondering what life would have been like if I'd taken my chances as a musician. That possibility frightened me. I may have walked around with my nose in the books those first few weeks at A&T, but my head was in the clouds. I constantly thought about getting out on the road.

Although I was barely eighteen years old, I already thought of myself as a professional musician, more or less, since I'd been steadily playing music (and making money at it) for the better part of a decade. So I spent my time after class strolling around Greensboro, poking my head into all the local clubs, and getting a feel for the music scene. Some players in town, especially at the jazz clubs, could really *play*. It was a little intimidating, but I wanted to eventually find a band to start gigging with and was determined to get in with the best. To me, this didn't seem unrealistic. I wasn't cocky, you know—just confident.

Instead of putting myself out there right away, I decided to approach finding a band like I had initially approached learning the piano: before I played a note, I would sit back and observe first, especially when I was in the company of the other music students. I found myself reluctant to play to my full potential because I wanted to figure out how things worked in the music department first. Who were the really talented players, and where did I fit in? I wasn't about to get shown up by anyone or be labeled a "show-off" before anyone really got a chance to know me, and I didn't want to isolate myself right off the bat. As fate would have it, though, showing off is how a band found me.

It took about three weeks before I settled comfortably into school life—class in the morning and afternoons, marching band in the evenings. Even though I was technically playing my horn every day, three weeks was a pretty long stretch without a real gig, and I was itching to get out there.

When I got back to my dorm room one afternoon, I just cut loose on some funky riffs—*loudly*—right there with my door open. After weeks of going strictly by the book and playing only my marching-band parts, it felt good to just play what came naturally. As I blew through that reed, all the anxiety and stress of the transition from home to college came out in a frenetic, funky stream of consciousness.

After a few minutes, I noticed a few heads peeking through the doorway, so I kept playing. Before long a crowd had gathered out in the hallway to listen to me, so I kept it going for them a little longer. I could hear murmuring, hands clapping—it felt good to have an audience again. When I finished, the crowd dispersed as quickly as they'd appeared, but a young trumpet player named Hayward Harper, another freshman in the marching band, stuck around.

"Hey man, that was really good," he said, rubbing his chin like he was deep in thought. Hayward was playing it cool, but I could tell he was really impressed. "Let me ask you something. When you signed up for the ROTC program, did you go army or air force?"

Now, I thought that was the strangest thing he could have asked me at that moment, but I answered that I'd signed up for the Army program. Back then, every male college freshman had to either join the Army or Air Force Reserve Officer Training Corps (ROTC) program, and since I was a big John Wayne fan from all those old war movies I'd seen as a kid, I went Army. As it turned out, that would be a very important decision.

"That's good," Hayward said, rubbing his chin some more. "That's really good because, look here, man, I'm in this group, and the cat that heads it is the ROTC instructor for the army program. I can get you a gig if you're interested."

My little stunt had paid off.

Hayward and I sat down and talked music for a while. I told him about Ulysses and the Mighty Blue Notes back in Kinston, and he told me about his band in Greensboro, the Prophets. The ROTC instructor, a really bluesy cat named Sarge, was the bandleader and drummer. Hayward explained that Sarge looked out for the guys in his group and took it easy on them when it came to their ROTC obligations. This kind of situation was good for me, because I did enough marching with the school band every day and didn't need any more of that in my life. What I needed was a gig.

Hayward wanted me to meet Sarge right away, so he took me down to his office in the ROTC building for something of an informal audition. When we got there, we found him behind his desk going over some paperwork. He looked a little annoyed at the disruption, but Hayward immediately started talking me up, telling him how good I was and how he really needed to listen to me play. I unpacked my horn, trying to be cool, while Sarge just sat back in his chair scowling. His blank stare made me a little uneasy, but I figured he'd come around once he heard what I could do.

I picked out a quick tempo in my head and jumped right into some funky licks, fully prepared for Sarge to hop up from behind his desk just as ecstatic as Hayward had been. But as I played, he just sat there, looking me over without saying a word. Every so often, I would catch a glimpse of him out of the corner of my eye, just staring a hole in my forehead, his face completely expressionless. I couldn't tell if he was unimpressed, bored, or just deaf, so I just kept on blowing. I was determined to get a reaction from this guy, good or bad. Harder and harder and funkier and funkier, I kept it coming until I started to get a little light-headed from the effort.

After what seemed like an eternity, Sarge quietly picked up the phone and, without a word, dialed a number. As I continued to play myself nearly unconscious, he listened until the other party picked up. Then he held the receiver out toward my horn, still completely stone-faced. By now, I was really getting concerned. Who was on the other end of that phone? Sarge held the receiver out in front of my horn for a minute or two before he put the phone back up to his mouth.

"Didn't I tell you this was the year a sax player would show up?" he yelled into the phone over my playing, showing the first sign of emotion since I'd been there. "Didn't I *tell* you?"

The person he'd dialed up was the band's piano player and Hayward's older brother, Ray, who was apparently impressed with my style as well. Ray had graduated from the A&T music program several years earlier and was teaching music up at the prestigious Palmer Memorial Institute in Sedalia, North Carolina.

Sarge hung up the phone and smiled. He stuck out his hand and offered me a spot in the band right there. I couldn't have been more relieved. I shook his hand and accepted the gig; then I promptly collapsed in a chair.

I liked Sarge instantly. His given name was Harold Jordan, and he had been a paratrooper in the Eighty-Second Airborne out of Fayetteville before coming to teach at A&T. Sarge carried himself like a born soldier. He was a gung-ho, blood-and-guts, hard-nosed grunt all the way. His uniform was always crisply starched, his shoes spit shined to a mirror finish. You could have sliced bread on the crease in his trousers. Like Banks, Sarge had some serious style. He drove around campus in a beautiful rust-colored '58 Lincoln Continental that he kept as neat as his uniform. It was one slick, streamlined piece of work, with long tail fins and whitewall tires. On the way to and from gigs, I'd ride in it with him, feeling like the big man on campus even though I was still a freshman. Believe me, when you were in that car, you were *noticed*.

I knew I was in tight with Sarge when he started calling me "Bird," as in Charlie "Bird" Parker, after a few weeks. I think we hit it off so well because I was as serious as he was about music and not into drinking, smoking, or any of the other habits you can pick up hanging around nightclubs. The army had molded Sarge into a disciplined man the same way our parents had taught us to be "good boys." He could tell my focus was on the stage, and he appreciated that.

I've never looked down on anyone for what they chose to do offstage. Early on, I adopted the philosophy of "To each his own" when it came to other people's vices. I wasn't about to do anything I thought would disappoint my parents, but that didn't mean I had to disassociate myself from people who did. When offered, I politely resisted the invitation to drink liquor or smoke pot, but I didn't lecture anyone. If that's what they felt like they needed to do to, that was fine. I just never felt like I needed any stimulants to get in the mood; the music itself was always enough for me.

Still, being the shining example sometimes had its privileges. One weekend, when the band didn't have any gigs, I mentioned to Sarge that I was going to visit some friends of mine from high school who were attending Bennett College. Bennett is an all-girls school also located in Greensboro, and his ears perked up at the mention of it. He knew I was going to see some young ladies and was grinning from ear to ear.

"Why don't you take the Lincoln?" he asked as he tossed me the keys. "Go ahead, ride around. Have a good time today."

I stood there for a second, holding the keys in complete disbelief. This man *loved* that car, and he was loaning it to me?

I wasn't about to argue with him, though. I drove that car all over campus with the windows down, smiling at everyone. All I could think about was the look I was going to see on those girls' faces when I rolled up in front of their dormitory in that shiny new Lincoln. When my friend Joyce and her sister, Charlene, finally did come out of their building, they just stopped cold and stared, their mouths wide open. I must have looked like the cat that ate the canary in that thing.

After several months of meeting new people at college, it was nice to finally hang out with some friends from back home. Our senior year, Joyce and I were voted Most Musical, so she wasn't surprised to hear I was already working with an established band. We caught up with each other's lives as we cruised through their campus, honking and waving at anyone they even remotely knew. We were all just friends, but I have to admit I secretly had a thing for Charlene back then (and had since I was fourteen years old). She reminded me of Natalie Wood, the beautiful star of the film *West Side Story*. Charlene had those same smoldering brown eyes.

We rode around in style all that day and stopped for cheeseburgers at a drive-in. Having steady gigs again meant I had a little money in my pocket, and I didn't mind footing the bill. I was on top of the world that afternoon. I had cash, a beautiful car at my disposal, and two of the prettiest girls in Greensboro to keep me company.

After that weekend, Sarge didn't mind loaning me the car occasionally, probably because I'd returned his baby to him without a scratch and with a full tank of gas. At the time, I was still in touch with my high school sweetheart, Velma, who was a little more than an hour away attending North Carolina Central University.

I would borrow the Lincoln and visit her on the weekends here and there, although less and less frequently as the school year went on. Velma was very smart and as committed to her studies as I was to playing funky music. We wrote each other every week at first, but eventually the letters started coming every few weeks, and the weekend trips to see her became less and less frequent. We were both really attached to our new lives, and deep down I think we both knew we would eventually grow apart.

I wish I could say I was as committed to my classwork as Velma was, but that would be a lie. The time I put into practicing and playing with the Prophets that first year really took its toll. Getting in from a Sunday-night gig at four or five in the morning on Monday made it incredibly difficult to make it to class. Sarge would usually excuse me from reporting to formation with the rest of the ROTC class, which meant I could sleep in, but I was still expected to keep up with my regular coursework and attend lectures like any other student. Although the band gigged steadily, there were occasionally periods without much going on, and I would use that time to catch up on all my reading assignments and research papers.

As the year wore on, though, more and more of my school-work gave way to picking up my horn and heading out the door to make gigs. I somehow managed to maintain a decent grade-point average that first year and still get out with friends and take in a basketball game or a movie now and then. The guys in my dorm were really great cats, but they could also be really crazy. One day some of them would not shut up about who the fastest guy in the dorm was. After a while, the arguing and bragging carried on to the point that someone was either going to have to put up or shut up. I told those guys about the time in high school when I raced the best guys on the track team and smoked every last one of them in the hundred-meter dash. (What I didn't mention is that I was so out of breath afterward, I had to decline an immediate rematch.) My dorm mates weren't convinced, though. You would have thought the answer to all the bragging would have been to organize an old-fashioned footrace and settle things once and for all, but it wasn't. These guys thought up a much more elaborate scheme that included going inside the corner store located a few blocks from the campus and shoplifting something. The idea was to intentionally get caught so that when you ran out of the door, the store's owner would try to chase you down. If you did it and got away, you would be recognized as the fastest guy in the dorm, hands down.

Now, I know shoplifting doesn't sound like the smartest thing in the world, but I accepted that challenge for some reason. It is one of the few times I can remember intentionally doing something my parents would not have approved of. Perhaps I felt like rebelling a little; perhaps I was just too eager to prove how fast I was.

Whatever it was, I walked into that little store and milled around for a bit before deciding on a travel-sized tube of toothpaste. As casually as I could, I slid the tube up the cuff of my shirt into my sleeve and held the end in my palm like some amateur sleight-of-hand magician. Remember, the idea was to get caught, and that is exactly what happened. The man from behind the counter yelled for me to stop as I approached the door, and I gave him one good step around the counter before I bolted. I looked back after I'd gone the better part of two blocks, and that poor old guy had barely made it out of his door to the street corner. I was back on campus and panting in my dorm room before he even made it to the end of the block.

Everyone thought it was really funny, and I basked in the attention briefly, but it wasn't twenty minutes before I felt this nagging feeling that I'd let my mother down. Someone once said the measure of a man's character is what he would do if he knew he would never be found out. I knew there was no way I would get caught for stealing that toothpaste and there was no way my mother would ever know, but that didn't change how I felt. Once the laughter died down, I went downstairs to make a phone call.

When the guy at the corner store answered the phone, he still sounded a little out of breath. I explained that I was the kid who had just been in there and ran out with the toothpaste. He was a nice man and politely listened to me as I apologized and offered to come back to the store and pay for the item.

"I'll understand if you ban me from the store, but I still would like to come by and make it right. My mother didn't raise me like this," I told him.

He agreed that it wouldn't be necessary to ever speak of it again if I'd come by and pay him, which I did. I learned that day that as fast as I could run, I couldn't outrun my conscience.

Around this time, the country was learning that it couldn't outrun its conscience either. The civil rights movement was in full swing by my freshman year in college, and North Carolina was right in the thick of it. In the fall of 1960, Kellis was one of four black students admitted to the University of North Carolina in Chapel Hill, a first at that university and very controversial. But integrating that campus was just the first step for Kellis, and during his sophomore year he organized demonstrations with other students to desegregate many of the campus's facilities. Segregation had a powerful effect on Kellis growing up, and throughout his life he worked tirelessly for social integration and equality. (He would eventually finish law school and go on to become the first full-time black professor at Columbia University in New York, something that I've always been incredibly proud of him for.)

The same year Kellis was admitted to UNC, four A&T students—Ezell Blair, Franklin McClain, Joseph McNeil, and David Richmond—seated themselves at the segregated lunch counter at a local Woolworth's in Greensboro and began one of the most important protest movements of the 1960s. They were, of course, refused service, but, determined to make a statement, they stayed in their seats at the white-only lunch counter. Within a few days, hundreds of students from the local colleges—black and white—had joined them. The kids were pelted with all kinds of food, had milkshakes dumped on their heads, and endured endless insults from an aggressive mob for weeks. Still, day after day they showed up in shifts and blocked the lunch counter, refusing to leave until they were served. They stood their ground and inspired one of the most massive nonviolent protests of the decade, and I have a lot of respect for them and what they went through.

Another A&T student was impressed by their actions—a freshman by the name of Jesse Jackson. When I met Jesse in 1961, he was very active in organizing peaceful civil disobedience in Greensboro. The Woolworth's lunch counter in Greensboro had already been desegregated by that time, but Greensboro had become a major hub of the civil rights movement. Jesse organized marches and other peaceful protests my freshman year, and I attended when I could. I marched, sang, and carried signs with the other students, enduring the insults and assaults to the point of having some mystery liquid poured on me during one march. I hoped it was just water, but something deep down told me it wasn't. Despite it all, I tried to carry myself with the same kind of dignity that my mother had always shown. By the time Melvin joined me at A&T in the fall of 1962, the civil rights movement was a runaway train, and my family was at the heart of it all in one way or another.

Still, I had obligations with my band that kept me from being as involved as I could have been. I told myself from the very beginning that I would do everything that I could to support the civil rights movement—except going to jail. That was a line I wasn't willing to cross. During one sit-in I attended, the police came and gave everyone ten minutes to disperse or we'd all be hauled off. As much as it bothered me to do it, I left. I had a gig that night and was not going to jeopardize the band. I was fully committed to the cause, but there was a practical side of life that I couldn't ignore. While the marches and protests were about black empowerment, a real sense of personal empowerment came with earning my own money. Having enough to send back home from time to time really meant a lot to me. My mother came to the campus for a parent weekend that year, and I was able to put some money in her hand when she left. I felt sorry for my roommate because he hardly ever had any gigs and had to borrow some money from his mother. I liked making my own way, and playing music made that possible.

In 1962, guys like Ray Charles and Sam Cooke were tearing up the R&B charts. Booker T. and the M.G.'s, an integrated band, had a funky little record out that year called *Green Onions*. I was learning a lot of this music, especially the Ray Charles stuff. Melvin and my cousin Tim, who had also come to A&T, formed a band called the Ultimates and got a steady gig as the house band at a familiar stop for touring groups, a club called the El Rocco. It seemed like every weekend, acts like Ruby and the Romantics and Little Willie John were there and, as part of the house band, Melvin got some great exposure backing them up. Although Melvin and I had played together our whole lives, we both enjoyed the opportunities to play with other musicians and gain some new perspectives. Still, whenever we did pick up the occasional gig together, that familiar groove would reappear.

In the fall of that year, Melvin, who had started classes at A&T, entered himself in a freshman talent show and asked me to accompany him. We didn't play any particular tune—we just got up there and clowned around like we were little kids again. We riffed off of each other and improvised, mostly. I don't think he won, but the crowd certainly responded to what we did. After that, people on campus started referring to us as "the funky Parker brothers." This new nickname was fine with me, because by that time Melvin and I had sort of dedicated ourselves to the path of being 100 percent funky.

By the end of my sophomore year, our reputations had grown to the point that if someone in town had work for a horn player or drummer, and the gig wasn't a straight-ahead jazz gig, Melvin and I usually got the first call. One afternoon a call came from a young man in need of a band for a show he'd booked in Greensboro the following week. The guy said he had been told about us while rooting around campus for some musicians. Of course, Melvin and I recognized the name right away. Marvin Gaye had his first big hit that year with "Stubborn Kind of Fellow," featuring Martha and the Vandellas on backup vocals. Melvin and I put together a band and rehearsed at the club with Marvin a few times before the actual show, learning tunes like "Hitch Hike" and "Pride and Joy." It was real work getting all that music together in a few days, arranging everyone's parts, plus getting all Marvin's signals down. There really wasn't a lot of time for hanging out and getting to know each other, unfortunately.

The night of the gig everything went off without a hitch, and I was stunned at how incredibly smooth Marvin was onstage. It was obvious why he was becoming a big star, and I knew he was definitely headed somewhere in the music business. At the same time, we did a great job stepping in and backing him up, and it dawned on me that big things were happening for me . . . and Melvin too. After all, here we were, backing up one of the rising stars of R&B—a gig we'd gotten solely on our reputations.

After the show, Marvin thanked us all, paid us, and left town. Some ten years later I was backstage at a show of his in New York when he came out of nowhere to thank me for doing such a great job at that gig in Greensboro. Someone had told him where I was, and when he found me, he gave me this giant bear hug that nearly lifted me off the ground. We would see each other occasionally on the road after that and would always laugh about that first little show.

In the spring of 1963, midway through my sophomore year, I was on top of the world. I had been introduced to a girl named Diane, and just about everyone I knew considered her the prettiest thing on campus. She seemed to be interested in me, and I was very taken with her from the beginning. We mostly just talked a lot at first, had lunch in the dining hall, and walked to class together—innocent little things like that. Eventually we traded our meal books. You couldn't get in and eat at the dining hall with someone else's meal book, so this swap ensured that we'd find each other if we wanted to eat that day. Diane was from upstate New York and had a different way of speaking and dressing; she had an urban attitude that made her a complete departure from the country girls I'd known in high school. She was a lot of fun to be around, not to mention incredibly attractive, and after a few weeks, lunches turned into riding around in Sarge's car in the afternoons and going out on dates at night. We started seeing a lot of each other for a while.

Diane was not a shy girl and before long made it clear that she wanted to take our relationship much further than I was comfortable with. As pretty as she was and as persuasive as she could be, I still was more into playing funky music than anything else. I still had that "take it slow" mentality that I'd developed in high school, and I wasn't ready to play with fire yet for fear of being burned. Diane wanted to have a more adult relationship and, in many ways, I was still that little boy from Kinston, North Carolina. My slow approach didn't sit well with Diane, and by the time summer rolled around, I could tell her interest was waning. Her response was almost what I'd expected, though; I knew from the outset that she was really drawn to the fact that I was a saxophone player and not as much to me personally. I knew I wasn't a jock or a hunk, so this explanation was the only one that made sense to me. She wanted to be on the arm of someone popular, and I fit the bill.

One evening I dropped her off at her dorm, and she'd apparently had enough rejection.

"You know, my little sister is coming to school here in a few years," she said as she swung the car door open angrily. "She'd be really good for you."

Diane got out of the car, walked inside, and that was that.

Despite the way it ended, I really treasure those times. You're only young and innocent like that once in your life. Still, as much as it stung, I knew I'd made the right decision. I had friends in high school who had gotten themselves into trouble by getting involved in relationships they weren't ready for. The way I saw it, if you got someone pregnant, you married them and started a family. I wasn't ready for that kind of responsibility yet.

I didn't know it at the time, but my carefree college days were almost at an end. Things were about to become much more complicated.

When summer arrived, I didn't want to pack it in and head back to Kinston. By this time Melvin and I had developed a whole new level of confidence in our musical abilities; it wasn't arrogance, but the knowledge that we could play our style of funky music with just about anybody. Heading home for the summer meant we could pick up gigs around Kinston with Ulysses, but I was itching to try something new. I'd been working on my sound and was developing a concept for my music, something that would really set me apart from everyone else. The prospect of heading up north and covering some new ground was irresistible, so when classes let out, I headed to the East Coast to stay with my uncle Bobby, who was living in Newark.

Bobby had a little band that played around town, mostly at a neighborhood place called Collins' Bar. I wasn't familiar with all of the tunes they were playing, so a lot of the time I'd just sit in whenever they played a blues tune or a standard that I knew. I was really starting to get into playing jazz, and there were some great clubs in Newark. I had gone out to some of the traditional jazz spots in Greensboro, but they were nothing like what was going on up there. Being so close to New York City, the jazz mecca of the world, meant a lot of spillover, and plenty of great players came out.

One night I poked my head into a club that was hosting a jam session and decided to sit in. I wanted to test my jazz chops, but I didn't know the changes to many of the tunes. When it was my turn, I would call a blues in B flat or F—a safe bet. I played pretty well, but I just couldn't believe the number of saxophone players in there waiting for a turn to play. Some of those cats were really talented, but almost all of them were trying to sound just like Charlie Parker. I decided I wasn't about to give up on my quest to find *my* sound, and if being a really great jazz player meant you had to go through a phase where you copied someone's style like that, I figured I'd wait. I'd learn "Ornithology" someday, but for the time being I was going to concentrate on the funkier side of life. So I headed back to Kinston.

It wasn't until I was back that I got some sad news from my mother. Banks had been wrenching around underneath his car one evening several months back when the jack slipped out and the Big M crushed him beneath it. I think my mother put off telling me because she knew how close he and I were. When she finally did break it to me, I was devastated for a while. Banks was more than just a teacher to me; he was a real inspiration, a father figure. He was the one I invited out to performances to see me play, the one who helped me pick out my college courses. We used to laugh and joke all the time and had so much fun together. I would have given anything to spend one more summer with him.

Mrs. Banks knew how close he and I were, and when I went to see her, she brought out his tenor, a Selmer Mark VI that'd I'd heard him play many times over the years. She gave it to me, saying that he always considered me his protégé and would want me to have it. Even back then, Selmer was the Cadillac of saxophones, and I'd wanted one ever since I found out that Hank Crawford and David Newman played them. If it was good enough for them, it was good enough for me. I've played on Selmer saxophones ever since, but my first one was especially dear to me because of who'd owned it first.

Melvin and I returned to A&T in the fall of 1963 more excited about our respective bands than about going to class. By that time, performing had become a bit of a distraction for me and was putting a strain on my grades. And the trip to see Ray Charles perform that semester solidified what I'd been contemplating ever since I got to A&T. I wanted to be a performer, not a teacher.

As I mentioned earlier, Ray was playing the Greensboro Coliseum, and at intermission I snuck around to the back of the building, hoping to catch a glimpse of the band. Something made me want to get as close to those guys as possible, and I figured I could catch them during their set break.

I was not disappointed.

As I walked under the covered loading area, the light illuminated the silhouette of a man I recognized immediately. It was Ray's saxophonist, Hank Crawford, leaned up against a support beam, smoking a cigarette like James Dean or something. He had on this caramel-colored leather jacket with matching boots; one leg was propped up on the pole, and I watched him take long drags of his cigarette. It was near midnight, and Hank still had his sunglasses on.

I stood and watched him for a while from behind another pole several yards away, exhilarated but too terrified to approach him. Here was the man I'd heard countless times on recordings, whose solos I'd listened to, whose approach I'd studied—I felt like I knew him. Still, all I could do was watch, in complete awe of his presence. He was the coolest thing I'd ever seen.

Before long, other members of the band spilled out and joined him—Fathead Newman, Marcus Belgrave, Philip Guilbeau, Bruno Carr, and Edgar Willis. As they stood around laughing and joking with each other, I couldn't help myself; I emerged from the shadows and, as casually as I could, inched closer. The band was more or less oblivious to my presence, as there were other people milling around back there too, but no one was more drawn to the band than me.

For a while I just watched, absorbing all I could. These men were the epitome of everything I wanted to be. College was becoming more of a burden, and I could feel the overwhelming pull into a career as a professional musician more and more every day. I wanted to be out where my heroes were, playing funky music onstage every night. It was a dream that was beginning to sound more and more plausible every day, and as I watched these men get ready to head back onstage, a thought crept into my brain. I'd followed them for so long and learned so much of their music. Now I wanted them to know who I was. I made a promise to myself right then to make that a reality.

"One of these days you're all gonna know me," I said out loud.

No one turned in my direction, so a little louder I said, "I don't know how, but some way, somehow, you all are going to know who Maceo Parker is."

I doubt anyone really paid much attention to me, but I meant every word. For me it was the swearing of an oath, a solemn promise that I had to give voice to in order to make it real.

I drove home that night, turning over in my head every possible way to start my career as a musician. I was not cut out to be a teacher, and I knew it. I was going to take the first big opportunity that came my way to break into the music business.

By this time, my life was a blur of classes during the day and gigs at night, many of them out of state. Most nights, after getting in late from a gig, I would head over to Melvin's dorm and check in on him before I went to bed. He and the Ultimates still had that steady gig at the El Rocco, but he was usually already in bed by the time my gigs ended. Still, I had that older-brother instinct, and I wanted to make sure that he'd gotten in safely. It was a club, after all, and sometimes fights would break out—you just never knew.

One night after coming back from a gig in Virginia, I stopped in to check on Melvin. I found him wide awake and grinning from ear to hear.

"Man, you're not going to believe this," he said. "I met James Brown tonight and he offered me a job!" I could tell by the look on his face he wasn't exaggerating.

As it turned out, James Brown had been in town for a gig with Ben E. King and Otis Redding that night, and afterward everyone went to the El Rocco for something to eat before hitting the road. Melvin told me that, during the set break, the club's owner, Mr. Faucette, told him that James Brown wanted to speak to him. Melvin was shocked but went up and introduced himself anyway. After some conversation, James offered Melvin a job with his band right there on the spot.

When James learned Melvin was in college, though, he immediately amended his offer.

"I'm not going to tell you to drop out of school," he told Melvin, "but if there is a time when you're *not* a student, you'll have a job with me. You have my word."

Back then, James Brown was very much into black empowerment and didn't want to interfere with Melvin's education. Songs like "Don't Be a Dropout" were meant to inspire young black students to stay in school and achieve independence through education, to create their own opportunities in life.

Melvin shook James's hand and told him he'd keep that offer in mind. The guitarist for the Ultimates, Jimmy Bethea, was offered a job by Ben E. King that night.

Melvin was understandably very excited about the prospect of joining James Brown's band. It was 1963, and James was in his prime, absolutely *killing* audiences every night with the most dynamic, explosive stage show around. It didn't hurt that he also had an incredible band to back him up.

It was the opportunity of a lifetime for Melvin, but my father didn't see it that way. He wasn't nearly as thrilled about the prospect of his son running off with James Brown and insisted that Melvin stay in school, which he did begrudgingly. My dad was taken aback by the whole situation, but I, for one, wasn't surprised that James would like Melvin's style of playing. Still, we were committed to finishing school, even if we were missing a little more class than usual.

As my junior year wore on, though, skipping class occasionally for a gig became more and more frequent and finally got to the point where I was barely keeping up with my course work. The siren song of the stage was slowly pulling me away from the classroom. I wondered if I was making a huge mistake by staying in school. The more I thought about it, I realized I didn't need a degree to keep playing the way I was playing. Besides, I was getting more of a musical education each night onstage than I was in the classroom. By the time school was out for the summer, Melvin and I had almost stopped going to class altogether. We discussed it and eventually decided that it was a waste of our time and our mother's hard-earned money to keep on that way. We would take a break from school for a year or so and come back when we were more focused and ready to be dedicated students. We wanted to see how the music industry worked, and naturally our thoughts turned to James Brown and his offer to Melvin.

Now, I knew how good Melvin was, and I was confident that I had what it took to be in James's band also. If Melvin was going to go hit up James Brown for a job, I wanted to take my chances as well. That summer I went to Newark briefly to play some gigs with my Uncle Bobby, then back to Kinston to pick up some work with Ulysses. By then we'd established that when Melvin and I came back to town, whoever Ulysses was using for sax and drums would just have to be "off" for a few gigs. It was steady money for a few weeks while Melvin and I tried to track down James and the band. When we heard James was going to be at the Greensboro Coliseum, we headed back almost immediately. We knew of a boarding house in town for musicians and got ourselves a room there and eventually took a gig with a local band that was staying at the house as well. Our idea was to make a little traveling money because we just *knew* James Brown would hire us. We didn't tell the band about our plan to get on the road with James because, first of all, they wouldn't have believed us. Second, if it didn't work out, we didn't want to talk ourselves out of a steady job.

On the day that James finally came to town, we got up early and didn't tell anyone in the house we were leaving. We rode over to the Coliseum in the car our dad had given us and drove around the perimeter of the building for a while until we spotted the buses. After a while a long, black limo pulled up, and we knew that had to be the man, so we parked the car and hustled over. When James finally stepped out of the car, I was struck by how he carried himself. He was impeccably dressed and made up; the shine on his shoes would have made Sarge envious. His hair was processed and perfectly styled. He was a short man, only about five-foot-six, but he wore heels that gave him another inch or two. He carried himself as though he were royalty, which in a way I suppose he was.

Melvin approached him first and reintroduced himself as the drummer James had met at the El Rocco. James recognized him right away and became really excited. He threw his arm around Melvin and started introducing him around saying, "Hey, remember that kid drummer I was telling you about? Well, this is him. This is Melvin Parker."

I was so proud of my brother; I almost couldn't believe the way James was fawning all over him. I followed closely behind them, careful not to lose them in the shuffle. It was obvious Melvin was in, and I didn't want to miss my chance. After a few more introductions, Melvin reminded James of his offer of a job if Melvin weren't in school. James, true to his word, hired him on the spot. I gave a little cough to remind Melvin that I was still there, and he pulled me over and introduced me to his new boss.

"Mr. Brown, I'd like for you to meet someone," he said. "This is my brother Maceo, and he's a great saxophone player. He needs a job, too."

James's eyes kind of narrowed and he looked me over, then looked back over to Melvin, who had this look on his face that suggested he might not join the band if James didn't hire me as well.

"I don't really need a saxophone player," James said slowly, almost to himself. "Let me ask you something," he said, seeming to reconsider. "Do you play the baritone?" James's previous baritone player, Leroy Fleming, had recently been drafted, and he needed someone to take his place.

Now, I knew there was only one right answer to this question. I pictured myself answering "no," and I could see the conversation ending right then and there. I wasn't ready for that, so I gave the only answer I could to keep things going.

"Er . . . yes, sir, Mr. Brown," I said.

He could have asked me if I played the saxophone standing on my head, and I would have still answered the same. This wasn't an outright lie, because I had played a little baritone sax in high school during the Christmas holiday once when Banks needed someone to fill in. Still, it was a bit of a stretch.

Then James asked if I *owned* a baritone sax, to which I replied with an equally hesitant, "Err . . . yes." He could obviously tell I was bending the truth a little and just smiled.

"I'll tell you what," he said, after thinking it over for a second. "If you can get a baritone sax, then you can have a job, too."

I stood there in complete shock and disbelief for a second. I couldn't believe what I'd just heard. At the end of that sentence, my brother and I were members of James Brown's band! To make it official, James shook our hands and sealed the deal—we were hired. *Both of us.* I wasn't excited about playing baritone necessarily, but I figured with a little patience I might get the chance to show what I could do on tenor someday.

Melvin and I were so overwhelmed with pride we must have walked a foot taller that afternoon. We were invited in to check out the show that night and were given tickets to some great seats where we could see everything. I took my seat in the audience, but James took Melvin by the arm and led him down to the stage while the road crew was setting up and began introducing him around. When one of the drum kits was assembled, James asked Melvin to go over and play something. He was obviously anxious to show off his new prodigy to the other guys in the band. Melvin went over and laid down something really funky, which brought a big smile to James's face. He was obviously thrilled with his new hire. "Man, didn't I tell you about this kid," he kept saying over and over, slapping people high fives and stomping his foot along with the beat. I felt a great swell of pride watching James make such a fuss over my brother.

That night we watched the show from out in the audience and imagined ourselves onstage there. Otis Redding was on the bill that night, although he didn't have a band. He did two songs, "These Arms of Mine" and "Come to Me." Both were in the same key and nearly the same song, but he was *killing* people with them, and I thought to myself that if this guy ever got a band, he was going to be unstoppable. James was really on that night as well. Melvin and I watched the way he moved, hitting with the band before he dropped down into the splits then came back up, spun around, and grabbed the microphone stand right back on the one. It was an amazing performance, and to think that we were about to be a part of that soon was almost too much. As impressive as the performance was, a lot of James's tunes were actually pretty simple. Melvin and I analyzed the set that night, dissecting what the band was doing, and realized we could do what these men were doing just as well, if not better. We were anxious to get onstage and prove it.

There was still the little matter of finding a baritone sax, though. I had no idea how or where I was going to get one. When we got back to Kinston, my mother helped me get one from Pierson's Music Store, where our family had been getting our instruments since high school. We didn't have the money to buy one outright that day, but when Mr. Pierson heard who had just hired me, he worked out an installment plan with my mother. I left the store that day and started working on my baritone chops.

Our parents, of course, would have preferred we stayed in school. But they had monitored our progress from the start, from the time I started piano lessons, and knew what Melvin and I were capable of. They also knew they'd raised us with a sound upbringing, and if we saw this as a good decision, they would support it. They were incredibly proud of us and couldn't resist telling their friends the news. We couldn't either. As great as it felt to tell people that we'd been hired by one of the biggest entertainers in the country, we hadn't actually gotten onstage with James yet, so Melvin and I were very anxious to get on the road. After about a week in Kinston, we were ready and met the band in Virginia.

James wanted Melvin in the show immediately. To be a horn player in his band, though, you had to know the routines and have the kind of dancing rhythm to keep up as well as play. We'd done routines like this in the Junior Blue Notes, but James wasn't convinced. I was told my job would be to sit in the audience and just observe for a while. I knew I could pick it up in no time and was incredibly excited to load my stuff on the bus that night. It wasn't the kind of bus that bands normally tour in today, with a lounge area and bunks. It was your standard Trailways bus with two rows of seats; each person in the band got one side of the aisle with both seats to himself. I realized right away that there was a certain pecking order on the bus, designated by where you sat. Melvin was assigned a seat right up in the front, and I was put way in the back. I didn't really take it as an insult, though. If you were on that bus, then you were part of the band, and that was all that mattered. I knew what I was capable of, and it wouldn't be long before my seat assignment would improve.

We rolled out of the parking lot and drove on through the night as everyone around me slept. I sat up wide awake that whole night listening to the sound of the bus, wondering what might lie out on the road before me.

4

All Aboard the Night Train

One of the first things I did after being brought onboard with the James Brown Band was to buy a little notebook. My thought was to write down at least one important thing that happened every day for a year or so. I wish I'd followed through, because it would have helped me write this book, but as it turned out I never wrote one single word in that journal. Things were happening too fast for that.

But despite the pace, I still had to wait for my chance to show what I was truly capable of. I was hired to play baritone sax, and there weren't many opportunities to solo. It wasn't that being part of the band wasn't enough for me. I just really wanted to play tenor, and more important, I wanted to solo on the tenor. I had a feeling that I would be able to prove that I was a serious tenor player, to contribute something unique, when the time was right. I just had to be careful not to overdo it.

James involved Melvin in the show right away, first sitting him down and running through all of the songs to get a feel for how Melvin played them. James liked having a variety of drummers, including Nat Kendrick and Clayton Fillyau (whom James called "Biggun"), for the different types of songs in the show, because he didn't feel one drummer could do everything equally well. One might play all of the ballads and another all of the slow swing numbers. Obie Williams did all of the up-tempo jazz tunes, and Melvin was there to play the funky stuff. This system of dividing up songs didn't mean the drummers could rest, though. They had to watch James at all times because he might signal one of them in the middle of a song, and they had to come in without messing up the groove. You had to be *on it* to be in James's band. After listening to Melvin play for a while, James picked out the tunes he wanted him to perform, and that was that; Melvin was in the show.

Things didn't move that quickly for me in the beginning. Learning the music for the show was only part of the job, as it turned out. The horn players also had intricate step routines worked out for each song that I needed to learn before I could get onstage, and they were all different. You had to have some serious dancing rhythm to keep up with these guys, so James told me my first job was to just sit in the audience every night and observe until I got those steps down. I told him that it wouldn't be a problem because we'd done routines like this with the Junior Blue Notes, but James wasn't convinced.

"Just because you *say* you can do something, doesn't make it so," he told me. "You just sit in the audience and watch for a while."

So I did just that, and after a week or so I was slowly integrated into the show. I think I surprised James with how quickly I picked up everything, but to me it was just natural. Melvin and I knew we could contribute to the band right away. By that time we had been playing together for such a long time that we could dissect everything about the show and figure out what worked well and what we felt we could improve on. Melvin wanted to "clean up" the funk. His concept of funky drumming was a little different than Clayton's or Obie's, and James obviously liked it. Melvin injected a new, youthful energy into the group.

I really wanted to play tenor, but I was very cautious in the beginning. I didn't want to appear ungrateful for the job, and I certainly didn't want James to get the idea I thought I was too good to play baritone. Still, I knew I wasn't going to be up there playing some funky solos as long I was on "the big horn," as James called it. Truth be told, a lot of James's songs, like "Try Me," were very simple tunes, and some of the stuff the band was doing back then didn't impress Melvin and me much. We knew we could play this music as well as, if not better than, the guys already in the band.

What *was* impressive was the way the band grooved on these simple tunes and brought it all together into a really dynamic performance every night. James was thirty-one years old—right in his prime—and was killing people with his explosive energy onstage. When all the turns, splits, and hits came together with the band, it was nothing short of incredible.

James's charisma both on and offstage was infectious, and the women loved him. My popularity with my female acquaintances skyrocketed once they knew whom I was working with. The girls who paid me no attention when I was a student in the A&T marching band became somehow "attracted" to me. I was fine with that, even liked it. I had always been very cautious in relationships and, regardless of all the newfound attention, I was still most comfortable traveling in the slow lane when it came to women.

It always came back to the concept of being a "good boy" for me. Anytime I even contemplated doing something risky, I thought about how disappointed my mother would be if I got myself in a bad situation. Being good didn't mean I had to live in a cage, but I found that doing the things I knew I was "supposed to do" limited my exposure to unforeseen dangers. For instance, when I began dating women I met out on the road, my number-one rule was always to rendezvous at the hotel; meeting a woman in a strange city at their place was just too risky. I'd heard stories of guys who were lured up to a woman's apartment only to find a couple of guys waiting there to rob them, and I wasn't about to let that happen to me. I learned a lot just by observing the older guys in the band and listening to their stories.

Until Melvin and I came aboard in 1964, the trumpet player, Ron Tooley, was by far the youngest in the band. He told me many years later that he noticed how the energy level really took off when Melvin and I joined. We bonded with Ron instantly and later with guitarists Jimmy Nolen and Alfonzo Kellum, whose nickname was "Country." The five of us had so much fun on the bus laughing and joking around—everything was funny to us. Onstage Melvin and I would have to keep from looking at each other during the show because we would just crack up laughing for no reason, especially in the really serious parts, like when James was on his knees singing "Please, Please, Please." Everything was new to us and incredibly exciting. At night I couldn't sleep and would sit up with the bus driver, a guy by the name of Bill Butler, just to have someone to talk to.

The one older cat in the band I really admired was St. Clair Pinckney. He was James's main tenor player, and he really had his head on straight. St. Clair was only thirty-three at the time, but he carried himself well, so I listened when he spoke. Some of the other guys would take a shot or two before performances, or drink a little on the bus if we had a long drive, but drinking and drugs really weren't a big problem in the band in those days. Since I didn't drink, I had to find other ways to relate to the guys. For instance, I bonded with the Flames—Bobby Byrd, Bobby Bennett, and Lloyd Stallworth—over music. We all really liked Otis Redding and would listen to his records together in the hotels at night.

Everywhere we went at least one person in the group knew somebody in town who could show us around a bit. Having a friendly place to drop by was really important because segregation was still prevalent, and there weren't a lot of places available to us, especially when dinnertime rolled around. If you were black in 1964 (a member of James Brown's band or not), you had to get your meals from the backdoor of the kitchen much of the time. The dining room at most restaurants was "white only." The bus station was the only place we could count on consistently being served, so if someone knew of a place "across the tracks" where we could sit down to eat, we were there.

Segregation was just the way of the world, so we were used to these conditions. We all *hoped* for change, but we accepted reality. In other words, it was insulting but not surprising to see a sign in a window that said WHITE ONLY. (In fact it was more surprising *not* to see a sign like that, and if that happened, you were a little leery of that place!) My experiences in high school playing for the white college students at the pickle warehouse in Faison had given me a glimpse of how the world could be, though. The idea that things could be different made it difficult to comprehend racism and segregation when I was confronted with it, because I *knew* people could coexist peacefully.

Touring some of the places in the South made me realize how behind the times and out of place segregation was. The audiences at most of the places we played up north were made up of a real mixture of people, even at traditionally black venues like the Apollo. It felt good to see them getting their groove on together, and it gave me hope that total integration in America could be achieved. James Brown's group was a cultural force bringing all different kinds of people together when so many forces were driving them apart. Melvin and I came aboard the "Night Train" just at the right time to participate in this phenomenon.

Segregation may have been an insult, but there were more dangerous elements in the South for young black musicians. For this reason, everyone in James's band carried a gun. Carrying a weapon was something new to Melvin and me, but we went along with it. I had a small .38 caliber pistol I kept in my waistband, although the most use it saw was shooting at bottles and cans when the bus would stop out in the desert somewhere and the band would have "target practice" to kill the time. Still, a few times we needed those pistols for real.

Once a club owner in Knoxville, Tennessee, refused to pay James after a show. After arguing with the man for a minute, James came back to the dressing room, fuming.

"You all come on with me, and bring your guns," he said.

I was scared half to death, because I had no intention of ever using that pistol on anyone. Something told me to get rid of the thing, so after everyone filed out of the dressing room behind James, I slipped out the back and hid my gun in the alley. By the time I got back inside, the club owner had paid James the money he owed him but had also called the police in the process. They must have been nearby, because they already had the entire band lined up against the wall and were escorting a few of the guys to jail. After everything was over, I went back outside and found my pistol. Carrying it was a fraternal thing with the band; it symbolized the bond that we all had. People throw around the expression "I've got your back" all the time, but in that band, we really meant it.

Situations like that were unusual, though, and for the most part, everything went smoothly on the road. After a few months with the band I began to settle into the touring routine, which consisted of long stretches of one-nighters all over the country punctuated by weeklong engagements at places like the Apollo Theater in New York City. The one-nighters were hectic because, between the traveling, rehearsals, and the show, there was very little time to do all the little things like getting your suit pressed for the next day before it was time to leave. It was exciting to see all these new cities, but it was a constant grind. Just when I started to feel burned out from all of the constant traveling, though, word would come down that we were doing a two-week stint at a theater somewhere. Then there was time to relax and catch up on all the little things because you had a home base to operate from: your hotel room. You didn't get your own room until you had been in the band a long, long time and had proven your worth, so Melvin and I usually roomed together.

After several months the band's touring patterns became familiar to me, and pretty soon everything became a carbon copy of the previous trip. The rehearsals, however, weren't always scheduled at the most convenient times. If something went wrong in the show, James would sometimes call a late-night rehearsal following the last performance. After playing five or six shows a day at the Apollo, the last thing you wanted to do was stick around and play "Try Me" one more time. (Tuesday nights were the worst because it was amateur night and, in addition to our regular shows, we had to rehearse with those people all morning and then back them up that evening.) But if James wanted to rehearse at midnight, then that's what we had to do. We also made several trips to the recording studio. The first recording I played on was "Out of Sight," which came out in September 1964. I may have only played the baritone part, but the enormous swell of pride I felt upon walking into a diner and hearing it come on the jukebox was overwhelming. I thought, That's me playing on that record!

Hearing that song on the jukebox solidified my feeling of belonging in the band. I was becoming more involved in the show and really feeling comfortable onstage. (Years later Ron reminded me of a time when he looked down the stage and caught me playing the baritone while sliding across the stage on one foot the way James would do. James must not have seen it, or I would have been fined for sure.) But as much fun as I was having, I was beginning to feel that it might be time to express my interest in moving to tenor. Besides St. Clair there were two other tenor players in the band—Eldee Williams and Al "Brisco" Clark—but James really only liked St. Clair's solo work. As luck would have it, I didn't have to wait very long for my big break.

St. Clair became sick and had to leave for a week or so to rest up. James looked a little worried about the situation, so I approached him and let him know I could fill in for St. Clair.

"Mr. Brown, I can play all those solos on tenor," I said. "Tenor is really my main instrument."

James must have seen in my eyes how badly I wanted it, because he only pondered for a second before agreeing. That night onstage, I pulled out all the stops and played as funky as I could whenever I was given a solo. Afterward James came to me and told me how good I sounded.

"Good Lord! You weren't joking," he said, slapping me on the back. He was genuine with his praise, and I could see that he was looking at me a little differently.

That night opened a new door for me. Over the course of the next few shows, I proved that I really had the chops to play lead tenor in the band. Just before St. Clair was set to rejoin the group, James pulled me aside and told me which songs he really liked my soloing on. When St. Clair returned he and I were going to trade off baritone and tenor on certain songs. Just like the situation with the drummers, James now had two tenor players he could count on. In the span of a few short months, my status in the band had risen substantially.

What really set things off for me was one very important recording session. "Papa's Got a Brand New Bag" was recorded in late 1964 for King Records. James had done some recordings for Smash Records and, owing to a dispute with King, Smash was barred from releasing any recordings of James's voice. So when he finally returned to King, the stage was set for a smash hit, and that's exactly what we delivered. When Melvin and I had joined the band, we injected a new, youthful energy into the mix that James was picking up on. His music was changing, becoming tighter and funkier, and James wanted to capture this new sound (hence the title of the song). What came out of that session is widely regarded as the birth of funk music.

Recording with James was always a loose affair. He would come up with a concept for the song and hash it out with the bandleader, whose job was to work out parts for the band. James was very paranoid about people stealing his lyrics, and he would jot down notes on bar napkins or scraps of paper—rough outlines that only really had meaning to him. This kind of informality meant that when the light came on in the studio and it was time to record, you really had no idea what he was going to do. The song itself was a simple blues, but the emphasis was really on the drums and bass. The horn lines were punchy and infectious; you couldn't help but hum right along. No one really knew who was going to play the saxophone solo since that hadn't been discussed, so, much like onstage, we all watched James for some kind of cue. When the time came, James uttered a phrase that would forever change my life.

"I just want you to blow, Maceo. Hey!" he screamed into the microphone.

I played my first recorded solo that night and laid into it like there was no tomorrow. When that record came out later the next year, my name was everywhere. That phrase really stuck out on the recording, and the name Maceo just stuck in people's heads. When I went into a diner and heard *that* song playing on the jukebox, I could actually hear *my* playing out in front, and it was an incredible feeling. The phrase "Maceo, I want you to blow" was so catchy that James started using it during the show because it just sounded cool and people picked up on it. My father, Maceo senior, would drive around the streets of Kinston, and people would pull up next to him and say, "Maceo, I want you to blow," and he'd oblige them by honking his horn. In a few short months I had risen out of an obscure spot in the band and become one of its star attractions. My life would never be the same.

Coming up out of incredible poverty, James Brown had had to endure more than his fair share of humiliation, so he put a premium on self-respect and expected everyone in his organization to conduct themselves in a dignified manner at all times. When you were in the James Brown organization, you represented him, and he took that *very* seriously.

No one called each other by their first names (at least not when James was around); everyone was Mr. Parker or Mr. Brown. He didn't tolerate drinking or drugs on the bandstand, which extended to the wings and backstage. We were expected to keep our clothes neat and pressed and our shoes shined at all times and to know what uniform the band was wearing onstage that night and have it ready to go. If the band was wearing bow ties, you'd better have your bow tie. If the band was wearing cummerbunds, you'd better have your cummerbund ready. James would have these little surprise "inspections," and I learned early on to rub Vaseline all over my shoes to keep them looking shiny. You only got caught with your pants down once or twice because James would fine you five to ten dollars for these types of infractions. Missing a note or losing a step onstage meant fifteen or twenty dollars came out of your pay. Somehow he was able to keep track of all these fines in his head, and after a show, he knew what everyone owed down to the last dollar. I didn't particularly care for this practice, but I have to admit it was an effective tool for keeping such an enormous operation running smoothly.

Still, there were times when James's discipline stretched beyond keeping his band in line and bordered on the ridiculous. Once somebody was complaining that the bus never parked close enough to the hotel and it wasn't fair that we had to walk so far with our luggage and instruments. This comment got back to James, and the next day he had the bus stop at the CITY LIMITS sign on the outskirts of town. We were all a little confused, but after a few minutes a car pulled up alongside the bus. James got out, boarded the bus, and addressed the band.

"Our agreement was that I'm supposed to provide you transportation to the city," he said. "Well, we're here at the city. Now *you* find your own rides to the hotel—and you'd better be ready for rehearsal on time." The band endured this punishment for several days until the offending party apologized to James for complaining.

For all of his good traits, James could be extremely vindictive and petty. He was paranoid about people talking behind his back and had eyes and ears all around who reported back to him. One of these "informants" was the band director at the time, Nat Jones. Nat was from Kinston like Melvin and me, but the guys in the band couldn't believe we were from the same town, because our temperaments were so different.

One particular incident almost ended Melvin's and my ride aboard the Night Train. Several months after joining the band, we were on our way to Minneapolis, up late on the bus talking about the previous show. We were probably annoying the people who were trying to sleep, but we were so excited we couldn't help it. I was doing a pretty good James Brown imitation, mimicking some of the phrases he said onstage, because it used to crack up Melvin. I wasn't making fun of James, just being a kid and clowning around.

The next day at the theater, James's wardrobe lady and assistant, Gertrude, pulled us aside.

"Mr. Brown wants to see you two. Nat Jones went and told him that you two were picking at him on the bus."

We went into James's dressing room and attempted to explain the situation, but James wasn't having any of it. He just stood there patting his hair down, threatening us.

"The next time you want to talk about me, you better have your guns ready," he said, getting right up in our faces.

Melvin, who has been known to have a short fuse, got right back in James's face.

"Oh, you mean this?" he said, reaching into his jacket. "Well, I've got mine now."

That admission made James back up, because he wasn't accustomed to anyone, least of all the college boys with the Christian parents, talking back to him. I could see the potential for the altercation to get out of hand, so I tried to defuse the situation.

"Listen, Mr. Brown, if this is the way it's going to be, then we don't have to be part of the show. We'll play tonight, but after that we'll just be on our way," I told him.

James didn't think we were serious, but Melvin and I packed our things the next day and headed back to Kinston, where we stayed for about a week until James called to apologize and asked us to come back. After that, I noticed he treated the two of us with a bit more respect. I don't mean to give the impression that crazy things like that happened all the time, but I was beginning to see a darker side of James Brown.

By the time the war in Vietnam was getting serious attention in 1965, I had been with James's band for about a year. Despite the disrespect I received at times, I realized that it was harder than I imagined to walk away from that kind of lifestyle. When you arrived somewhere like the Apollo Theater and had the red carpet rolled out for you, it made the endless bus rides and the late-night rehearsals worth it. I was getting used to being recognized for my solos and was intensely proud to have a seat on that bus. A year was more than enough time to become accustomed to being a big part of the hottest band in show business.

So imagine my shock when, one afternoon, a letter arrived at my mother's house in Kinston that said I was supposed to report to the army induction center at Fort Jackson, South Carolina. I didn't want to believe that the Vietnam War was going to end my ride on the Night Train, so I immediately tried to devise a way to stay out of the army and remain in the band. I had seen enough of those old war movies to know how the military operated. No matter what James put us through, at least he didn't wake us up with a bugle call at the crack of dawn (although I wouldn't have put it past him).

Back then, everyone knew about a few ways to get out of the draft. If you had a severe enough medical condition, you were exempted. But I was in great shape, so faking some kind of illness or affliction wasn't going to work. If you had some political connections, you could get into the National Guard and avoid combat, but I wasn't the son of a US senator or anyone like that. You could also get a deferment from the draft if you were enrolled in college full-time and making progress toward your degree. Going back to A&T would have kept me from the war, but it would also have kept me out of the band, which defeated the purpose.

Eventually word got around the band that I'd received a draft card, and almost immediately everyone began to approach me with one crazy idea after another to keep me out of the service. When James heard the news, he called me over and suggested that I get married.

"Don't you know someone we could make a deal with?" he asked me. "You know, make some sort of arrangement? Maybe we could pay them a little something. Don't you know anybody?"

The truth was I certainly knew a girl or two I could approach with the idea, girls who wouldn't be terrible to be "married" to temporarily. I noticed very early on how many young women would come to see James Brown. Groups of pretty young women were always hanging around behind the performance hall after the show or huddling close to the bus. They were always eager to talk to musicians in the band, so meeting them wasn't difficult. Truth be told, it was nice to have a girlfriend in New York that I could see whenever we were somewhere like the Apollo. When we headed out West, I realized I could have a girl somewhere like Los Angeles who wouldn't ever find out about my girl on the East Coast. How would they ever run across each other? It was a great plan as long as none of these girls ever met.

Before long, that east-west thinking turned north-south, and I found myself with a girlfriend in the South and another in the Midwest who I would call on whenever the band came through. It was a great time, but I tried to keep everything at arm's length with these girls. I enjoyed their company, but at the end of the day, I was focused on playing music and not on starting a family.

One of the women I met during this time, however, would ultimately have a profound and lasting effect on my life. I first saw Carolyn Washington when she and her sisters, Jeanette and Sandra, along with their cousin, Ruby, formed the Brooklyn chapter of the James Brown Fan Club. We would play five, sometimes six, shows a day at the Apollo for a week or more back then, and I began to notice that these girls were in the front row for every show (and I mean *every* show). Carolyn and I would see each other outside of the theater after the show, and eventually we went on a few dates. Carolyn's family took to me right away, and I thought of her often while I was on the road. I didn't know it yet, but I had just met the woman who, in a few short years, would become the mother of my children.

But, at the time, marriage was the farthest thing from my mind. Still, when James mentioned the idea of getting married to keep me from going to Vietnam, I admit I seriously considered it. The idea bounced around in my head for a while, but as nice as these girls were, the thought of signing my name to a marriage certificate seemed more terrifying to me than going to war. What if something went wrong and she wouldn't give me the divorce when it was all over? I was brought up in the church, and when you got married it was for the rest of your life. I figured the war wouldn't last more than a couple of years. (Unfortunately, I was very wrong about that.)

St. Clair had the great suggestion to tell the draft board that I was a homosexual. He thought that was really funny, but I wasn't even going to consider that idea.

"Well, what if you were just plain stupid?" he said, still chuckling. "You know, unable to grasp any of the concepts they'd try to throw at you. Just, you know, dumb."

Between college, marriage, an alternative lifestyle, and playing stupid, this last option seemed like my best bet. Even if you were ensured of a deferment, everyone still had to go down to the local draft office to be classified. A 1-A classification meant you were prime soldier material and an ideal candidate for the service. As I rode the bus to the testing center, I made up my mind to be as far down the alphabet as I could get.

Things couldn't have started off better for me that day. As I boarded the bus to the induction center with the twenty or thirty other draftees, I noticed immediately that I stuck out like a sore thumb. A year on the road with James Brown had done wonders for my wardrobe. I wore a pair of neatly pressed slacks cut high up on the ankle to show off my Italian leather boots (which were shined to a mirror finish, of course). Up top I had on a collared shirt with a neat, waist-cut jacket like a matador would wear. I must have looked like a visitor from Mars compared to those other farm boys when I stepped off that bus at Fort Jackson.

After a physical examination, the military instructors administered the written test. I immediately realized that failing the thing wasn't going to be as easy as I thought. The army wasn't exactly looking for the next Albert Einstein. It sounds funny, but when you're asked absurd questions like, "What follows the number four?" you have to come up with an equally absurd answer if you want to fail convincingly. It's twenty-seven, right?

I went on giving silly answers like this for pages and pages—the more remedial the question, the more ridiculous my answer. Afterward I sat there awaiting the test results, trying to look completely mentally drained. I sincerely believed I had completely ruined my chances of becoming a soldier and was feeling pretty proud of myself.

Before long, a group of four officers, each representing a different branch of the military, came out to speak to everyone individually. My blood ran a little cold when the four of them came to a stop behind me and stood there murmuring to each other. After a few seconds of looking over my file, one of them spoke up.

"Parker, I want to talk to you about your test score here." He thumbed through the pages of the test, looking very concerned. "According to the test results, Mr. Parker, the only thing you're really qualified to do in the army is stand beside a stove and make sure the fire doesn't go out."

I almost laughed out loud at this statement. But I didn't want to tip my hand, so I choked back the smile that had started to creep across my face. I was still committed to playing the part of a total imbecile, and I had to look completely lost or at least apathetic if I was going to sell this. They looked me over for a moment before the officer with the files produced another, thicker file from his stack.

"Do you know what this is?" he asked. I just shrugged my shoulders, trying to look as vacant and confused as I could. "This is your cumulative folder from school. Let's see here, four years of high school, almost three years of college," he said, slowly flipping over page after page. "Wow, look at these grades."

I closed my eyes and thought about all those times I had tried to make the dean's list.

"Look at all this musical training you've had," he said, barely bothering to disguise his sarcasm. "You know, we have *military* bands."

Closing the file, he looked down his nose directly into my eyes, which by now were genuinely vacant from the onset of shock. He leaned in a little closer and spoke to me the way a concerned father would.

"Let me tell you something. Anytime you get a letter that says you have to report to a place like this and take a test, you're practically in the military already. All this here is more of a formality, really—a way for us to figure out where you need to go." He patted my shoulder and let this information sink in.

I didn't need to be told that being an army cook was a terrible assignment, and it was looking like that was my only option based on my test scores. The officers talked among themselves for a few minutes before explaining to me that I would be allowed to take another version of the test that day and, if my score was high enough, would be guaranteed an assignment in a military band. It was my best option if I didn't want to spend the next two years peeling potatoes. My heart sunk. For all my scheming, this entire thing had been out of my hands from the beginning, and the best I could do now was just avoid getting shot at.

I agreed to take the test again and was given a different series of questions. When the officers came back to talk to me the next time, they informed me that I'd not only passed, but made the highest score of the day. Afterward I left that room with their assurance that I'd be assigned to an army band right out of basic training. It was hard to be excited about playing in a military band, considering the band I was already in, but it was preferable to being shipped off in an infantry unit. I still had to come to terms with being drafted before I could see the bright side of the situation, and I thought about it the entire bus ride back to Kinston.

I made up my mind that day that if I were going to go in the military for two years, I was going to have fun and party the entire time. I had heard about guys going into the service and saving all kinds of money, but I decided I was going to make it my business not to have a dime by the time my tour was over. I called up James and let him know I was being drafted, and he said he understood the situation and wished me well. When I was finished with my tour, my job would be there waiting for me, he said. Even though I had that to look forward to, two years still seemed like an eternity to be away from the band.

5

Southern Exposure

The year 1964 was pivotal not only for Melvin and me but also for the world. In the United States, the passage of the landmark Civil Rights Act of 1964 promised to put an end to the segregation and discrimination that people like Martin Luther King Jr., Jesse Jackson, and my own brother Kellis had fought so hard to eradicate. That same year King was awarded the Nobel Peace Prize. On the other side of the coin, however, China exploded its first atomic weapon, forever shifting the balance of power in the world. Later that year, the U.S. Congress passed the Gulf of Tonkin Resolution, which gave Lyndon Johnson the power to effectively wage war in Southeast Asia and assist the government of Vietnam in repelling any communist invaders. In a strange way, the year that signaled the end to a violent and shameful period in American history also marked the beginning of a new one.

That year saw another more peaceful invasion with the arrival of the Beatles on American shores in February, followed by the Rolling Stones later that summer. The "British Invasion" was soon in full swing and threatened to overshadow traditional American music acts, including James Brown. In October, however, a significant movie was produced to announce to the world that

American music wasn't about to roll over and die in the face of this new musical craze. *The T.A.M.I. Show*, or Teen Age Music International (also known as the Teenage Awards Music International), was an all-star event that featured Chuck Berry, Jan and Dean, Smokey Robinson and the Miracles, the Supremes, Marvin Gaye, and James Brown and the Famous Flames. Headlining the show were the Rolling Stones, riding high on the release of their eponymous debut album. I really wanted to play that show, but James couldn't take everyone in the band. I watched the entire program on television that night. With Melvin drumming, James put on one of the best performances of his life and upstaged the red-hot Rolling Stones. (In later interviews, Keith Richards referred to following James Brown that night as one of the worst career moves the band ever made.) The Brits were invading the American musical landscape, but American artists weren't going down without a fight. Our band had thrown the first counterpunch.

By the time the fall of 1965 rolled around, I'd gone from being the big man on campus at A&T University to playing alongside one of the greatest figures in music to being a tiny fish in the great green sea that was the US Army. Because of my work on "Papa's Got a Brand New Bag," the name Maceo was everywhere, and I wore it proudly like a badge.

A few short months after that hit record came out, though, I had to trade in that badge for a name tag sewn on a uniform that simply read PARKER. Still, I knew my self-worth wasn't tied to whether I was wearing polished wingtips or spit-shined boots. I was more than just a name called out on a recording. And when it came to the military, I was *certainly* more than just my name, rank, and serial number, which is what we had been told to believe comprised us.

When I arrived for basic training at Fort Gordon near Augusta, Georgia, I was given the MOS—military occupational specialty—title of 02L20, which is simply the army's convoluted way of saying "saxophone player." Augusta was James's hometown, and I had been through there plenty of times with the band, so I was pretty familiar with the area. My training was scheduled to last eight grueling weeks, but I discovered that it was actually fairly simple and straightforward once you got used to it. I got out of bed when the drill sergeants told me to get out of bed, ran when they told me to run, and jumped when they told me to jump. If they told me to stand in a room full of tear gas, I did. If they told me to belly crawl under barbed wire through mud while holding my rifle while live ammunition was being fired over my head, I did that, too. More important, I did it all without asking any questions, which I discovered was really the secret to making it through.

I realized early on that the entire basic training program is a harsh indoctrination designed to occupy nearly every minute of your time, partly to keep you from dwelling on your situation and partly to brainwash you. Eventually you find yourself in a place where you don't think and instead simply follow orders. Every day you are broken down by the physical exertion and lack of sleep, then built back up by mastering the soldiering skills you are taught.

I found I particularly excelled on the rifle range. During our first trip there, I scored very high on my marksmanship qualifications and earned some serious praise from my drill sergeants. My eyesight was pretty good back then, and it seemed like I could hit anything I aimed at. Once I realized I was distinguishing myself as a good marksman, though, I decided to be a little less accurate from then on. I thought if I were too good with that rifle, the army might conveniently forget the arrangement I'd made and put me in a position where I'd have to use it for real.

There wasn't much free time during my training, and on the rare occasions we were given a weekend pass to leave the base, I stayed behind. I didn't see any sense in torturing myself by pretending I was free for a day or two. If being part of a military band kept me out of a lot of running and crawling through mud, it also meant a lot of long rehearsals (which James's band had readied me for). My time with Sarge in the ROTC during my college years prepared me for all of the marching and hiking, but at the end of the day basic training was a stressful time, and I was glad when it was over.

Eight weeks at Fort Gordon came and went in a blur, and before I knew it, I was moving on to the assignment that would occupy the next two years of my life. On the last day the drill sergeants marched the entire graduating class into a giant building and announced everyone's active-duty assignments. We all sat there in that room quietly sweating bullets as an officer read out each soldier's last name alphabetically followed by their next duty post. I thought about how the officers at my orientation promised me that I would be assigned to an army band, but I still had no guarantee that that arrangement would be honored at all.

As the names of my fellow graduates were read over the loudspeaker I prayed I wouldn't hear some far-off place in Vietnam called out after my name, which unfortunately is what a lot of those young men heard that day. To my relief, when "Parker, Maceo," was called out, "434 Army Band in Fort Gordon, Georgia," was what followed. True to their word, the induction officers had arranged it so I would stay in Augusta.

After the ceremony, we were all dismissed and given a week or two of personal time before we had to report back for our active-duty assignments. It was a really somber day for many of the guys I'd just spent the last eight weeks with, and I tried to contain my relief that I wasn't being shipped off to a war zone.

I was grateful to have some time off and went home to Kinston for a few weeks to spend some time with my family and try to get my head together after all that brainwashing. The first few months with James's band had been its own boot camp in a way, and living on the road for months on end was stressful in its own right, but it was an exciting and glamorous life and, frankly, I missed it. I was grateful not to be dodging enemy bullets, but life back at Fort Gordon looked like it might kill me with sheer boredom. Looking back, I laugh at how badly I underestimated what being drafted into the military during wartime will do to people. I thought the people I'd met out on the road as a musician were as strange as they came, but as it turned out, the guys who were drafted into the army with me in 1965 were some of the craziest people I've ever met in my life.

My first night back at Fort Gordon was a great example. I had left Kinston early that morning and had spent the entire day changing buses, waiting in stations, and wrestling with my bags. I was exhausted when I finally arrived at the base late that night and was assigned to my bedding in the barracks right away so I could get some sleep. One of the clerks led me to a darkened building full of sleeping soldiers, and I was escorted down the aisle between all of the cots and eventually shown to an empty one at the end of the row. I put my gear down as quietly as I could and crawled under the covers. Almost as soon as my head hit the pillow I drifted off.

It felt like I'd just fallen asleep when I heard someone in the room begin to shout. "Oh, no! Oh, God! No!"

I sat up and looked around wildly for the source of the screaming, but I was the only thing moving.

"It can't be time to get up yet!" the voice shouted. "I ain't even *peed* yet."

I sat there in the dark waiting for something to happen, but nothing did. No one else seemed even remotely alarmed at the commotion that had shaken me from my well-deserved sleep. Finally a few of the soldiers yawned and stretched but for the most part seemed completely oblivious to the ruckus coming from the far side of the room. Was this a normal morning for these guys?

After a few minutes, I made out the shape of a figure moving toward me in the predawn light. It was a soldier dressed only in his boxer shorts, a T-shirt, and combat boots. The guy was duck-walking down the aisle between the beds making a rhythmic, almost dance-like shuffling sound with his feet. On his head he wore his combat helmet without the canvas straps that attached to the inside to keep it from falling down over your eyes and covering your entire face. The helmet came down nearly to his chin and bobbed back and forth in time with his shuffling. The clinking of his helmet and the shuffling of his boots made a lot of racket, but even in the dark it was obvious that he didn't care. As he passed the stirring bodies in their bunks, he turned his head to greet them, his helmet swiveling wildly.

"Good morning, Whitey," he said cheerfully to a white soldier who was just waking up. Without missing a beat, he turned to the bunk on the opposite side of the row. "Good morning, Blackie," he said to a black soldier who sat up and rubbed his eyes. The duck-walking figure kept this up all the way down the aisle, shuffling his feet and greeting the waking soldiers based on their ethnicity. "Good morning, Whitey. Blackie, how are you this morning?" No one really paid any attention to the guy, but I couldn't stop watching.

When he finally reached the end of the row, he stopped and lifted up his helmet slightly. In the dim light, I could make out two bulging eyes peering down at me.

"New!" he shouted, pointing directly at me. "Hey, guys," he yelled out. "Check it out. New!"

When no one responded, he turned back to me and smiled. "What's your name, New?" he said in a sarcastically tender, almost paternal way.

I didn't know *what* to think. Was this guy completely insane? I didn't answer and just sat there completely dumbfounded, watching as he plopped himself down on the edge of my bed like he belonged there and began to inspect my gear. He lifted up my boots, examining them as if he'd never seen a pair before.

"New!" he yelled out, holding one boot up to the light. He unfolded my trousers and held them up for inspection before fondling my helmet for a minute. "Ooh! New," he said again, stretching out the word into a long, melodic syllable. I still didn't say a word.

By this time, a few of the other soldiers had gotten up and were stumbling around groggily, brushing their teeth and dressing themselves. "New!" he said again and again, repeating it to the soldiers who happened to amble by my bunk as if it were some kind of weird introduction.

This strange little ceremony went on for several minutes before I was saved by the morning call for everyone to roll out for formation. The crazy soldier dropped my things, made a beeline for the locker by his bed, and began to get dressed. I did the same, but by the time I put on my uniform, I'd lost sight of him in the frenzy of all the soldiers moving around.

As the platoon gathered outside for morning roll call, I stared in amazement as it became clear that the guy who'd woken everyone up was my actually our *squad leader*, a guy by the name of Mashburn. He wasn't the highest-ranking guy in our unit, but Mashburn, or "Rico" as he was nicknamed, was certainly in a position of authority, and that scared the heck out of me. If this crazy guy was our squad leader, I tried to imagine what the platoon sergeant must be like.

That first day was hell, and I wanted to strangle Rico by the end of it. During my time in the band at Fort Gordon, though, he and I eventually became pretty good friends, and to this day he remains one of the craziest, most hilarious people I have ever met.

Rico was a drummer in the band and just about every day would do one crazy thing or another to keep things from getting too serious. Every week the band had to get all shined up and march for a basic-training graduation ceremony. Once Rico switched up the standard marching beat we were supposed to play and started tapping out some kind of Caribbean-sounding rhythm on the snare drum with just his fingers. After a few measures the cymbal player switched up his rhythm a bit and fell in line with what Rico was doing, and by the end of the march the entire band went from sounding like a military marching band to Harry Belafonte's backing group. Our company commander was a good sport about it and just shook his head. I suppose he recognized the monotony of it all and was grateful for a bit of humor.

Another jokester I met later on in my army career was a guy we nicknamed "Neck" because of his incredibly long neck. He had the strange habit of singing everything he wanted to say (at least when he wasn't addressing someone in a position of authority). Neck would walk by me in the chow hall in the morning and sing a soulful hello or croon about how tired he was after a particularly grueling day. ("Sweet" Charles Sherell, who played bass for James Brown after I returned from the army, knew Neck from back home, and we laughed and told stories about that guy constantly.)

After a while, I began to see a million fascinating stories in just about every one of the guys I was stationed with. A young private by the name of Harrison, whom everyone called "Pie" for some reason, was the brother of the famous musician Wilbert Harrison (who wrote the hit song "Kansas City") and was himself a musician. We gigged in several bands while we were stationed together, and whenever we meet up now we laugh about all the great times we had. I was certainly very wrong about my time in the army being dull. How could it be? We were all young men forced into a situation that none of us wanted to be in, and consequently we did everything we could to make life as normal as possible. Guys like Rico and Neck kept everyone laughing with their crazy antics, which ultimately distracted us from dwelling on the monotony of army life and the dread of seeing combat. As much as I did to improve my situation, as much as I tried to keep to my promise of partying and having a good time during my service, at times my thoughts returned to the life I was ripped away from and where I *really* wanted to be. The guys who lifted my spirits were a real blessing.

The schedule in the regular army was more relaxed than the basic-training regimen. We had weekends off, and I was determined to get a gig as soon as I could, so shortly after arriving back at Fort Gordon I went around to all the nightclubs and hot spots in Augusta to check out the scene. Before long I found a band I really liked called Leroy Lloyd and the Swinging Dukes. Leroy was a hot guitar player, and the band did all of the popular tunes of the day as well as some really funky original material.

Again the name Maceo preceded me, and Leroy was really agreeable to having me join. The Swinging Dukes were pretty well established as one of the premier bands in Augusta and gigged regularly every weekend. Occasionally there were gigs out of town and I traveled with the band as far away as Florida to play shows. Our company commander made it clear from the outset that gigging on the weekends was OK as long as we remained in the state of Georgia. Crossing state lines was not allowed, but I never really adhered to that rule. As long as I was back on base by Monday morning, ready for duty, I didn't see why Uncle Sam should interfere with my music. I jumped right in with Leroy and his Dukes and was encouraged to solo on any of the tunes I liked. Eventually I started improvising elaborate introductory vamps that led into the songs. I wasn't necessarily the star of the show, nor did I want to upstage anyone, but I was treated like a special guest each night and given a lot of latitude to play what I felt.

One thing that began to emerge at this time was my stage presence. At some point I took it upon myself to start introducing the band and interacting with the crowd during the show, something that I hadn't had the opportunity to do much of before. It wasn't that I wanted to steal the limelight, but quite honestly, someone needed to have a rapport with the crowd, and I took the initiative. No one had any objections, so I continued to effectively emcee our shows, and before too long I became very comfortable in that role. I didn't know it, but I was preparing myself for my return to James's band, where I would eventually pull double duty as emcee and performer night after night.

In the area around Augusta, Leroy and the Swinging Dukes were established enough to pick up gigs backing touring artists who were without a band, much like Melvin and I had done for Marvin Gaye back in college. Otis Redding, who had blown me away the previous year, was making his way through Augusta and had hired Leroy and his band to back him up for a few shows. Otis was already well-known (especially in his home state of Georgia) for his first big hit, "These Arms of Mine," and had added several more songs that were destined to become classics. He had really hit his stride as a performer. I was knocked out by his energy and his incredibly powerful voice. To this day he remains one of the most dynamic and unabashedly soulful performers I have ever seen.

After eight months of marching in the 434 Army Band at Fort Gordon, I received word from my commanding officer that

I would be transferred to another base. A saxophone player was leaving another unit and I was being sent to fill in. I wasn't told where I was going at first, and initially I hoped I would be sent to Fort Dix in New Jersey. Being stationed there would have put me close to Carolyn in Brooklyn and my uncle in Newark. When my transfer orders came in, however, I was assigned to Verdun, France—about as far away from New Jersey as you can get. I was a little disappointed at first, but almost immediately I thought it might be a thrill to travel abroad, something I had never done.

France was incredibly exciting. From the moment I stepped off the plane, I tried to use what little French I remembered from high school. I could count the money and greet the people I met, but my French was honestly really, really bad. Still, the French seemed to like that I made a genuine effort. Sadly, I barely had time to dust off my French before Charles de Gaulle, the country's president at the time, kicked all non-French troops out of the country. France was becoming more independent and wanted to take responsibility for its national defense, so all American and NATO forces were asked to leave. The American government obliged, and within a few weeks I was trading in my "*Bonjour, mademoiselle*" for "*Guten tag, fraulein*" and boarding a train headed for Bremerhaven, Germany.

I was incredibly disappointed by this sudden turn of events. Paris had a great reputation for its jazz scene, ever since guys like Dizzy Gillespie, Charlie Parker, and, later, Miles Davis started performing there. I hadn't heard a thing about Bremerhaven's music scene. Not long after arriving, though, I discovered that one of Germany's premier jazz bars was right on the Rickmerstrasse. Chico's Place, an American-style jazz and blues club, was an important tour stop for jazz musicians as well as a meeting place for Germans who loved American music and for Americans (predominantly soldiers) who needed a little slice of home. Almost immediately I hooked up with a trumpet-playing ex-pat and began gigging there.

William McKay, or "Mack" as everyone called him, had been out of the service for a few years when I met him in 1967 but had married a German woman and decided to remain in Europe and play in the jazz scene there. He was a big fan of Freddie Hubbard and played just like him. He also wrote and arranged for a big band; he was a very talented guy, and we hit it off immediately. Mack's band did mostly jazz standards like "It Might As Well Be Spring" and "Body and Soul," and I had a lot of fun with those guys. I made twenty German marks each night, which wasn't much in those days, but since I wasn't drinking my pay away (which a lot of the guys did) it added up over time. It wasn't really about the money. It was about stretching out musically, having fun, and doing what I was born to do: play my horn.

As before, my name preceded me in Bremerhaven, and some people came out to see me play because they knew who I was. A wink and a smile from a girl in the audience let me know I was popular in my own right, but I was always careful not to step on Mack's toes onstage. It was obviously his gig, and he was the star of the show. Mack was really popular with all of the military guys who played at Chico's but was also very well connected in the jazz scene around Germany. It wasn't long before he was introducing me to other musicians and hitting me up to play out-of-town gigs with him and mostly German cats in places like Bremen. One group we played with off and on was a British group who nick-named me "J.B." because of my association with James Brown. (When they said it, though, their thick London accents stretched it into "Jay-Bay"). I really fell in love with Bremen, and over the years I've probably played there forty times. (I don't think I ever went back to Bremerhaven, unfortunately. I hear Chico's is a Russian dance club these days.)

Before I really knew it, my discharge orders came. I had begun learning German; I was also experimenting with writing band arrangements and was toying with the idea of having my own group. Truth be told, I was having so much fun in Bremerhaven I considered staying in Europe and playing music there when it came time for me to either leave the army and return to the United States or reenlist. I knew I could keep the music going like Mack had done. My job with James Brown would always be there, so it wasn't like I needed to hurry back before the "offer expired."

Ultimately, though, the thought of being just another workaday musician brought me back home. If I got back out on the road with James, I would have a little more status than the average musician. In Germany, I would just be someone who once played with James Brown—and, honestly, so what? I'd kept in touch with Melvin during my time in the army and knew that he planned to return to James's band when he got out. (Melvin had enlisted not long after I was drafted and was stationed in Vietnam doing communications work—a pretty dangerous assignment, as it turned out.) He had a little less than a year to go in his tour of duty, and the thought of being on the big stage and playing with Melvin again appealed to me as well. My mind was made up. I said goodbye to Bremerhaven, to Mack, and to Chico's, and boarded a plane bound for North Carolina. True to my word, I didn't have a penny to my name.

6

Keep the Fires Burning

Shortly before I left the army, I was reassigned to a mail-distribution office in Bremerhaven for several months. I went from hauling around my saxophone with the band to hauling giant bags of mail and unloading them off of giant sea/land trailer trucks. It was Christmastime, and there was plenty of mail to haul—tons of letters and packages full of Christmas presents—and hardly anyone there to do it. The heaviest thing was a bag filled with *other bags*. It was rough, but Uncle Sam made sure he got every bit of work out of me he could. When I flew home from Germany in the spring of 1967, I was ready to do just one thing—nothing.

I arrived in Kinston and moved in with my mother. I knew that I would eventually get back with the band, but before that could happen I needed to chill for a while and get my head together. I had two years of military life I needed to unwind from before I was ready to get serious again and get back onboard the Night Train. It felt good to sleep in for a change. I must have slept for days after I got back. I think eventually my lack of motivation started to irritate my mom. She began to make subtle suggestions about possible work I could find and, before long, just flat-out asked me if I intended on doing *anything* in the near future. My youngest brother, DeLond, had joined the navy by that time, so the house was relatively quiet throughout the day.

When I returned to the band in the fall of 1967, a whole new cast of characters had emerged, a lineup considered by many to be the best of all the incarnations of the James Brown Band. Two of James's legendary drummers, John "Jabo" Starks and Clyde Stubblefield, were there, as well as two new saxophone players, Waymon Reed and Alfred "Pee Wee" Ellis, who was the musical director. Pee Wee had studied jazz extensively and had even studied with Sonny Rollins in New York for a time; he impressed me immediately with his abilities as a player and as an arranger. One of the reasons James's band continued to get better was that new musicians were almost always brought on at the recommendation of somebody else in the band, which meant that they were already vetted, in a sense. When Melvin rejoined the band in 1969 after his stint in Vietnam, we talked about how the new guys could read the music so much better and how the dynamic was better too. Before the band had been composed of a lot of talented individuals, but this iteration had a sense of unity and cohesion that I hadn't felt before.

Another new addition was Fred Wesley on trombone. The first time I heard Fred play I knew instantly that we could play together. He was a great jazz player, and I could see how our styles would complement each other. You don't get that with everyone you play with.

I began taking on more and more responsibility in the band, eventually becoming something of a handyman. If we needed someone to emcee the show and do introductions, James would pass that job to me. James was great at shifting things around on a whim. If the road manager was absent, I was asked to help out getting things ready at the venue. Once James had a disagreement with the guy who did the comedy routine before the show.

"Man you ain't doing nothing," he told him. "Maceo can do *that!*" When the guy disagreed, James said, "Wanna make a bet?"

And, just like that, I was assigned the duty of doing the comedy routine without any training or experience, which I continued to do for quite a while. I was assigned a number of similar duties in the organization when the need arose, including the all-important introduction. I still remember that whole spiel by heart:

"Right now, ladies and gentlemen, it's showtime! Introducing the young man that you have selected as Soul Brother Number One! The man who sings 'Try Me'!"

The band would hit together on the one chord.

" 'Prisoner of Love!' "

The band hit again half-step higher.

" 'Papa's Got a Brand New Bag!' "

Again, another hit a half-step up.

"I break out in a 'Cold Sweat!' 'Get It Together!' 'I Can't Stand Myself!' 'There Was a Time!' Here he is with the world-famous Flames, Mr. 'Please Please Please' himself."

And the band would hold that last hit before I finally said, "James Brown!" The band would vamp, hitting on the up beat until James finally strode onstage and grabbed the microphone. Then, after James gave the drummer one quick look, the band would instantly start the first song of the show. It was showmanship at its finest, and it was really exciting to watch. The crowds went absolutely crazy for it.

I was elevated in the band hierarchy, but ultimately that meant a lot more responsibility. This type of "promotion" could be more trouble than it was worth sometimes. We would perform a number of Ray Charles tunes from time to time during the set, and James would sing these songs in his own style, which I liked, although I was always a much bigger fan of Ray Charles's voice (more than almost anyone's). The way that James did these songs was not the way Ray did them and not the way I would have done them myself. I will say that I have been blessed with a voice that, when it's on, can approximate Ray's. When it's really, *really* on, sometimes it can be scary. (I know it's on when no one in my band says anything after I finish singing.)

One song we used to do with James was "Georgia on My Mind." During sound check, I would take turns singing the lyrics with another cat in the band—one night he'd sing, and the next it would be me. He seemed to feel it was a perfunctory duty, but I really enjoyed it.

One night in Raleigh my voice was really on, and I went for it, channeling my best Ray voice and singing every word like it was a live show, not just a sound check. Afterward guys kept coming up to me and telling me how great it sounded.

"Maybe you should sing that one," someone said.

I was flattered. It didn't take long for word to travel because about a half-hour after sound check Gertrude came and told me that Mr. Brown was out on the stage and wanted to see me. The look in her eyes told me that it was a serious matter, so I dropped what I was doing and made my way to the stage. In my head, I thought that maybe James was going to give me something else to do in the show that night—maybe even a raise for all the extra work I was already doing. A raise turned out to be the farthest thing from his mind. I found him there by himself, ambling around, and asked him what he wanted to see me about. He acknowledged me and waited for a few seconds before he responded.

"Listen here," he said, "I got something to tell you. Are you ready for this?"

"Yes, sir," I said. I was ready for a raise, promotion—whatever he was about to throw at me.

"No, I'm serious," he said sort of smiling to himself. "Are you ready, *my* man? Are you ready for what I'm about to lay on you?"

"Yes, Mr. Brown. I'm ready."

He paused again, adding an air of dramatic flair to the whole exchange. I was starting to get a little confused.

"I can play the saxophone," he said flatly.

I stood there stunned. I thought maybe it was some kind of joke, but he didn't laugh. I knew damn well that James Brown couldn't play the saxophone, but if he said that he could, who was I to argue?

"Uh, yes, Mr. Brown," was all I could manage. I had no idea how to respond.

"I'm serious. I can play the saxophone standing on one leg," he said, grinning. "I can play it spinning around, all up on my back, down on my knees—all of that. If I started playing saxophone, you'd be finished. Do you understand?"

I told him that I understood what he was saying, but as I started to ask what his point was, he cut me off.

"I just wanted you to know that," he said with a smile and then strode offstage.

I realized that he'd heard about my Ray Charles impression during sound check and was not happy about it. James was fine with people in the band getting a little attention, as long as it never intruded on what he perceived as his realm. In other words, you better not for a minute give the impression you could do something better than he could.

Nothing more was said about the Ray Charles incident, and I thought things had gotten back to normal. But four or five shows later, at the end of "Prisoner of Love," I found out how funny about this kind of thing James could really be. The ending to "Prisoner of Love" could go on forever some nights if James wanted it to, the band just vamping and the backup singers singing "prisoner of love, prisoner of love," over and over again while he improvised. This night, though, he addressed the crowd directly.

"You know, the other day," he started, "I ran into Ray Charles."

My eyes widened. I knew instantly whatever was about to happen was directed at me, and I began to sweat a little.

"In fact, I think I saw Ray here tonight," he said. "Has anyone seen Ray?"

He looked back at the band, who just kept playing the vamp and doing their steps like they were supposed to, looking completely confused—me included.

"I know he's around here somewhere," he kept saying. "Ray! Hey, *Ray!*" He strode all around the stage as if he were really looking for someone. I started to get the feeling that he wanted me to do something, but I wasn't sure what. We were playing the vamp to one of James's songs, not a Ray Charles tune. But after a few seconds I knew he was calling me out to the microphone to show off my Ray Charles impression—*during the show.*

I started going through my catalogue of Ray's tunes, trying to think of something that would fit over the vamp. Finally James left the stage with the band still playing. As I walked to the front of the stage I thought of the words to "You Don't Know Me." In my best Ray voice, I leaned into the microphone.

"You give your hand to me, and then you say, 'Hello.' "

The crowd went crazy.

"And I can hardly speak, my heart is beating so."

This thing was really working, and the crowd was eating it up, but I didn't know how long I could keep it going. I thought, I need to get out of this, so I moved into "What'd I Say" but slowed down and to the "Prisoner of Love" beat.

From left to right: Bobby Bennett, Baby Lloyd Stallworth, Bobby Byrd, James Brown, John Starks, me, St. Clair Pinckney. New York City, 1964.

Back in James Brown's band, 1967.

Left to right: Me, St. Clair Pinckney, and Alfred "Pee Wee" Ellis. The James Brown band, 1967.

Dinner with St. Clair
Pinckney, 1968.
COURTESY OF ALAN LEEDS

Dong Tam,
Vietnam, with
Tim Drummond
on bass, 1968.
PHOTO BY AND COLLECTION
OF BERNARD C.
FEATHERSON

Maceo and All the King's Men, 1970. From left to right: Eldee Williams (tenor), Jimmy Nolen (guitar), me (tenor), Bernard Odum (bass), Melvin (seated; drums), Richard "Kush" Griffith (trumpet), Alfonzo "Country" Kellum (guitar and bass), and Joe Davis (trumpet). With the exception of Joe, Melvin, and me, everyone else has passed on. COURTESY OF ALAN LEEDS

In 1973 with Jimmy Parker (left) and St. Clair Pinckney. COURTESY OF ALAN LEEDS

Me at Charlie O's Queen Street, Kinston where Melvin worked, in 1974. AUTHOR'S COLLECTION

Byron Yoburn, Kellis, and me.
Chinatown, New York City, 1976.
PHOTO BY ELIZABETH TURNOCK

My brother Kellis and my mother, Novella.
New York City, 1976. PHOTO BY ELIZABETH TURNOCK

From left to right:
Me, Fred Wesley,
and Pee Wee Ellis,
1992. AUTHOR'S COLLECTION

With Stevie Wonder at the
Rhythm and Blues Foundation
Pioneer Awards, 1997.
PHOTO BY MARK BRETT

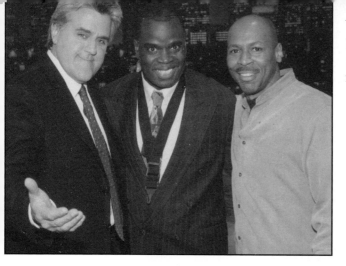

With Jay Leno and Kevin Eubanks, 1998. Photo by Natasha Maddison

With George Clinton at the Rhythm and Blues Foundation Pioneer Awards, 2003. Photo by Marcy Guiragossian

With Dave Chappelle in New York, 2004. Photo by Afshin Shahidi

With Jada Pinkett
Smith in Los
Angeles, 2005.
PHOTO BY NATASHA MADDISON

With Laurence Fishburne, Herbie Hancock, and Joni Mitchell. Los Angeles, 2005.
PHOTO BY AFSHIN SHAHIDI

At the Leverkusen
Festival in
Germany, 2007—
my Ray Charles
tribute.

Cologne, Germany, 2007. Photo by Ines Kaiser

On the island of
Réunion, 2008.
Photo by Tino

"See the girl with the diamond ring? She knows how to shake that thing—yeeeow!"

I ended the thing right there and walked off the stage too. From all the applause and cheering I could tell that the crowd absolutely loved it. I'm not sure if James was surprised by my performance, but he recognized the reaction it got, and soon the Ray Charles bit became part of the show. I never knew when it was coming or what song it would be part of, but when James told the crowd that he'd "seen Ray Charles the other day," I knew I'd better figure out how to work some lyrics into whatever we were playing at the time. What started out as an attempt to embarrass me turned out to be probably the most fun I had as part of the band. It taught me that you had to be on your toes and expect anything. You might be asked at the drop of a hat to do something you'd never done before, and you'd better be ready to jump right in.

It wasn't just me who had to be on their toes, though. The whole band got a shock one night in Los Angeles when Tina Turner showed up at the gig. James decided he would bring her out for one number, and the band was really excited by her presence. Tina was in her prime, absolutely incredible, and could really move. You could tell that she was in awe of James by the way she came onstage, but the minute she started singing (and especially dancing) all bets were off. At one point James did a hit with the band and Tina mimicked it. The band followed her as well and hit a second time. Then James did a spin and Tina followed with an identical spin. It was incredible! What started off as a tip of the hat quickly became a game of showmanship between the two. When James did a split, Tina followed with a split. When James kicked the microphone and brought it back, Tina followed right behind him. Move after move Tina followed whatever James did with amazing precision, adding her own little flair to it. The band was excited and really got into it—it was like watching two heavyweights go toe to toe.

Finally, after James realized that he couldn't shake her with any of his moves, he simply waved to the crowd and walked offstage. The place absolutely erupted! The band was equally stunned, and I was in complete awe. Tina kept the band going until a few minutes later James returned to the stage dressed in completely different clothes and lugging a suitcase behind him. He waved good-bye to the crowd as if to say, "I'm done. I'm out!" The crowd went crazy for this bit of theatrics, and it gave us a way to end the song. If I ever see Tina Turner again I have to bring this story up, because it was one of my best memories of performing with James Brown.

I don't mean to suggest that I was the only one who took on more than his share of responsibilities. St. Clair Pinckney had been part of the band long before I got there and remained long after I'd finally left. He was just as committed to making things work as anyone. He used to love driving the equipment truck from city to city. One night he made the decision to stay behind and help the driver make the trip between shows; we had a long way to go, and it was too much for one driver to do on his own. There was some trouble on the road, and the bus made it to the gig before the equipment truck did, so the decision was made to lease some equipment for the night because, after all, the show must go on.

I don't remember the exact circumstances, but I know that St. Clair tried like hell to get there in time and showed up a little after half of the show was over. The first thing he did was rush over and find out what everyone was wearing that night and then dressed for the second half of the show to make it to the stage. Later that night, someone called me over to tell me that Mr. Brown wanted to see me. I came in, and James told me point blank to relay the message to St. Clair that he was fired. I stood there, stunned. This man had given his life to James Brown—he'd been playing saxophone with him when I was only listening to the music on the radio. I tried to plead his case.

"Mr. Brown, the only reason he was late is because he was looking after our equipment," I explained. I knew that James didn't like that kind of thing at all. If he made a decision, he expected that you follow his orders without question.

"That is not his job, Mr. Parker," James yelled. "His job is to show up, on time, and play! Now go tell him that he's fired." James turned his back to me and went on with what he had been doing before I arrived.

I was crushed. But James Brown gave the order, so I knew what I had to do. As much as it hurt me, I delivered the message to St. Clair that night. James wanted him gone, and that was that. It was a terrible night, and it started me thinking about my future in a way that I hadn't before. If James could fire St. Clair, a man who'd been loyal for so many years, was anyone really secure? Though St. Clair was hired back shortly thereafter, I began to see things a little differently.

Carolyn, the girl I'd met in New York before I left for the army, had joined the band as a backup dancer, and we'd become really close during our time on the road together. Eventually we reworked the seating arrangement on the bus so that we could be next to each other every day, which worked out well because it meant a little more room for everyone else. Nobody was going to complain about that. We were nearly inseparable, and I loved being on the road with her. We used to try to make each other laugh during the shows the way that Melvin and I used to. When the band swung by New York City we would visit Carolyn's family, who took to me right away. Our time on the road together was cut short, however, when she found out that she was pregnant. She left the band in early 1968, and that summer our son Kevin was born.

Carolyn and I have spent nearly forty years together and have six beautiful children: Belinda, Kevin, Corey, Damon, Lashaun, and Kendra. When it comes to them, I've always tried to be supportive rather than influential, meaning I've never tried to push them into anything like music but just to be a positive and encouraging force in the things they want to do. I had always told myself that when I had a family, I would do everything I could to make sure they were taken care of. My parents made sure my brothers and I didn't have to go through a whole lot of craziness when we were growing up, and I was bound and determined that my children wouldn't either.

As far as material things went, we had absolutely nothing when we started off. We lived very simply, first in Brooklyn with her family and eventually in Kinston. I always felt that if we held it together, I would be able to provide for my family the way I wanted to. Before Carolyn came along, I thought that the magic formula for a successful family was to take that giant leap into marriage with a high school or college sweetheart and hope for the best. I learned, though, that there isn't a particular formula that guarantees you anything. The only equation that really balances out is one that factors in hard work. Both people in a relationship have to work hard at making things work, because it's too easy not to. Another thing I learned, however, was that the hard work was actually pretty easy when you have that *love*. When you have that type of real love that Carolyn and I do, it makes it easy for the two of you to shoulder the responsibility of raising a family together. I look back on forty years of marriage and six children who are all successful and have their heads on straight and feel a wonderful sense of accomplishment there.

In March 1968 I visited Africa for the first time as part of James's West Africa tour. As we got off of the plane that first day in Abidjan in the Ivory Coast, I heard the crowd chanting my name:

"MA-CE-O! MA-CE-O!"

I wasn't sure what to make of it at first. The more I walked around, though, I heard it more and more. A couple of times I heard someone saying it to a friend in passing.

"Hey, man, Maceo," a guy would say as he waved to a buddy. They were using it like the phrase "What's happening?"

The press picked up on this peculiar greeting right away and eventually explained to some of these guys that Maceo was a *person* in the band, not some kind of code or slang that James was using. These cats thought that my name was just something cool to say because James said it on his records. They figured if it was cool enough for James Brown to say all the time, then they'd say it, too. I don't think he found it very funny that the crowds were chanting my name that day, but I got a good laugh out of it.

The fact that my name, overheard on a record, could infiltrate a place's language showed me just how much influence James Brown had, not only in America but all over the world. This tour is widely credited with starting the soul movement in Africa, which later included the 1971 Soul Concert in Ghana and the concert that coincided with the 1974 Ali-Forman fight in Zaire. James was invited to official state dinners while we were there, and the band was treated very well. From traveling around, though, I saw, for the first time, how much inequity there was in Africa; poverty took on a whole new meaning for me when I saw the conditions that people lived in there. I wanted to interact with them, but it was incredibly difficult to bridge that cultural gap. I didn't speak French or any of the local dialects, and I certainly didn't understand any of the local customs. The last thing I wanted to do was offend anyone. It was strange to feel at arm's length from people I was beginning to feel a kinship with.

Being in Africa for the first time filled me with a strange mix of sadness and pride that I couldn't put into words. It wasn't until many years later, when I read Alex Haley's *Roots*, that I could identify the feeling. Being in the "motherland" gave me a great sense of fulfillment. When I returned to Africa in 1975 with James's band, we toured Senegal and went to Gorée Island, where slaves were housed until they were ready to be shipped off to the New World. We walked through these giant buildings that reminded me of the enormous tobacco warehouses in Kinston. I thought of all of the people who'd been there, shackled, waiting until the slave masters had met their "quota" and were ready to ship them out. I was overcome with emotion and to this day can't really find the words to describe it other than to say that it was a powerful experience. Black Americans were reestablishing ties to Africa—the idea of black power was taking hold, and I was proud of being part of that bridge back to the motherland.

The tour of the Ivory Coast was a great success, and I returned home in March 1968. Less than a month later, on April 4, the world was stunned by the brutal assassination of Dr. Martin Luther King Jr. in Memphis. An incredible wave of rioting and mayhem swept over the country that night. I was upset by the carnage but understood the rage behind it. I've never been one to get too involved in politics, but I knew the rioting was really a message: "You can't just kill our leaders and expect us to take this lying down." And on some level I could relate to their outrage. I didn't agree with the destruction and violence, but I understood where the anger came from. Still, Dr. King would not have wanted it. Violence gave the people opposed to black equality the "excuse" to respond with violence. Dr. King had been able to get things done without that. I had trusted his decisions implicitly; if he thought we should take up for striking workers somewhere, I knew that was the right thing to do. I didn't question his "whys" and accepted his vision. He was the one person who could have rallied our people to the right way of thinking.

We were scheduled to perform at the Boston Gardens the following night, but the rioting in DC and Chicago scared the promoter, and the show was nearly canceled, giving rise to rumors to that effect. It was decided, however, that there wasn't enough time to get the word out and canceling would just exacerbate an already tense situation. The mayor's office, the police, the show's promoter, and James got together and devised a plan to televise the show and perhaps keep people off the street that night. People were lining up at the box office to get their refunds when the announcement was made. It was an unprecedented event that would ultimately save the city of Boston from what would have been a terrible night of violence.

The show started off normally with the opening acts, and I was relieved to see that we weren't playing to an angry mob. Being the show's emcee involved a little comedy routine, some jokes and impressions to warm up the crowd before launching into the famous James Brown introduction. There was so much tension in the room I wasn't sure I wanted that job, especially with the television cameras on us.

As I walked to the microphone, I thought that, now more than ever, people needed a reason to laugh, and if I could be silly and tell some jokes, maybe everyone would forget about what had happened the day before, if just for a few minutes. I started off by doing what any good entertainer would do and complimented the crowd.

"We've got a nice-looking audience tonight," I said. There was almost total silence. "We do have a few ugly ones out there," I said, which got a little laugh. "They're split up, though," I said, and pointed around the room. There wasn't much laughter so I went straight into the comedy routine, first with a joke about a little boy and girl taking a bath together. The little girl points and asks what the little boy has "down there." The little boy answers that he doesn't know what it is or what it's for, when the little girl asks if she can "touch it." The little boy says, "Well, no! You done broke yours off already!"

This joke got a huge response, and I was relieved almost immediately. I did a whole bit about how I really wanted to be a singer but how singers always spit everywhere. The crowd was into it, which was a good sign. I followed that up with a joke about two guys, one who had a bad stutter.

"Two cats walking down the street, real fast," I said, and Clyde, on cue, started playing a quick shuffle on the snare. "The first cat says, 'Say, man, d-d-d-d-did you see that girl?'

" 'Where?' the second cat says.

" 'Aww, she's gone now,' the first cat says.

"They keep walking, and pretty soon the first cat says again, 'Say, man, d-d-d-d-did you see that girl?'

" 'Where?' the second cat says.

" 'Aww, she's gone now.'

"They keep walking for a minute, when the first cat says, 'Say, man, d-d-d-d—'

" 'Yeah, I see it,' the second cat says.

" 'Well, why did you step in it then?' "

This one brought down the house. Those people laughed harder than I'd ever heard an audience laugh. By the time I realized that things were going to be OK, it was time to bring James to the stage. I made one announcement about how several transportation routes were closed, and then I did the usual introduction with the band.

The rest of the show went off like dynamite. We started off with "Get It Together," which seemed appropriate. James called out, "Maceo, I want you to blow," in the middle of the tune, and I obliged while he danced and called out hits to the band. After a minute James called out for Jimmy Nolen to do "that Wes Montgomery thing," and Jimmy went off on a great octave solo on guitar. He even called on St. Clair to give a little baritone sax solo before we went into "There Was a Time." We did all of the James Brown hits that night, like "I Feel Good," "Cold Sweat," and "I Got That Feeling." Marva Whitney came out and did hits like Etta James's "Tell Mama" and her hit "Check Yourself."

At one point in the show, Mayor Kevin White addressed the crowd, calling on black folks and white folks alike to honor Dr. King's memory by conducting themselves following the nonviolent principles that Dr. King preached his entire life. It was fairly well received by the crowd, and it let me know just how important what we were doing that night actually was. We were keeping a city at bay. James probably helped the situation by giving the mayor an endorsement, calling him a "swinging cat" and asking for several rounds of applause for him.

The show was televised later that night and several times throughout the weekend in Boston and is credited with almost single-handedly quelling the violence in the city at a time when other major urban areas were tearing themselves apart. I gained a new appreciation for music's healing powers after that experience, something that has never left me and that has shaped the message and direction of my own music. Despite everything positive we'd accomplished that night, there was still the knowledge that we had lost our most important leader. We set out for Rochester the next day to the news that other cities across the nation were still in flames.

A month later, in June 1968, the band did a special USO tour in Asia, which included shows in Japan, Korea and, most important, several stops in Vietnam. The entire band wasn't allowed to travel to Vietnam, so James only took a select group with him that included me, Waymon Reed, Jimmy Nolen, Alfonzo Kellum, Clyde Stubblefield, our new bass player Tim Drummond, opening act Marva Whitney, and St. Clair Pinckney. We were affectionately called "the Saigon Seven."

I was given the added job of "military liaison," because of my military experience, which meant, in effect, that I was the band's road manager. I dealt with the soldiers in charge of loading our equipment, arranging our food and lodging, and transporting us around. It was a stressful experience at times but incredibly rewarding when we could see how badly those men needed some entertainment. As visiting dignitaries we were given honorary commissions as officers; we were also asked to wear military fatigues as a safety measure. We were given credentials, and my ID card had the honorary rank of colonel. The artificial rank was really just another safety measure for us if, for some reason, we were ever captured by the enemy—officers were treated better, apparently.

The army made all of our travel arrangements, and our safety was a big priority. They made sure we were well fed and had comfortable accommodations. Our helicopter transports included snipers by the door, whose job was to spot any possible attacks. The military is a well-oiled machine, and we were treated very well. Our equipment was another matter, though. Shortly after arriving I noticed all of our amplifiers, guitars, and drums were stacked up near the supply depot without anyone looking after them. This equipment was expensive, and it could have been damaged or, worse yet, stolen. I spoke with the supply sergeant and was informed that they didn't have anyone to *spare* who could guard our equipment. Instead I asked that they bring the equipment to where we were staying so I could at least look after it.

The band was staying at the Continental Hotel in the middle of Saigon, which was a really nice place, despite some serious damage the building had sustained from the fighting. Anything we needed was brought to us, because—for obvious reasons—we weren't encouraged to venture out.

One afternoon, though, boredom got the better of me, and I let our bass player, Tim Drummond, talk me into going out and exploring the city.

"C'mon man. Let's just go walk around and see what's going on," he said in a nonchalant way. "Let's just go get a souvenir or something and come back."

Before I knew it the two of us were hustling through the streets of Saigon, taking in the sights. The city was extremely busy, completely full of people pushing past each other on the sidewalk, dodging waves of bicycles and angry drivers stuck in traffic. We hadn't gone very far at all before I started to notice some people with bandages and injuries that looked like they'd been recently patched up. After a while, it occurred to me that there were a lot of these people around, some of whom didn't appear to be friendly at all. I noticed that some of them were staring at us intently with a mix of curiosity and hostility. I started getting a bad feeling about our little excursion. Tim and I had made a bad decision, and I knew the best thing was to get back to the hotel as quickly as we could. I realized how vulnerable we were. If things got ugly for some reason, we would have nowhere to turn. We settled on some souvenir ivory key chains and quickly made our way back to the hotel without incident.

For most of the trip, I never felt like we were in any danger during the shows, even though we could hear the rumble of artillery and occasionally gunfire off in the distance. Traveling was a different story, though. One night after a gig, as we were on our way to another base, our transport plane took some enemy fire. We didn't know what had happened at first, just that the plane started shaking and the cabin began to fill up with thick, black smoke. It was a pretty small plane, and the pilot just calmly turned his head and announced that there was "something wrong with the plane" and that he felt like we should turn back and land. We were all in agreement with that decision. It wasn't until we were back on the ground that we could see how badly the plane was damaged. I have to hand it to that pilot for being so cool and collected, although I doubt that was the first time his plane had been shot at.

Our last gig was at a place called Bear Cat, a giant base east of Saigon and home of the Ninth Infantry Division. The soldiers sat out on this huge hillside and watched the final show just like they were back home, except that there was the sound of artillery firing in the distance. As it grew darker out I noticed that I could actually see the tracers from the rounds being fired as we played. That night the fighting was closer than it had been at any other point on the trip. During one break a soldier came up and urgently handed me a note. It was a special announcement and, as emcee at the time, it was my job to inform the audience that "all the soldiers in Bravo Company need to report immediately." The perimeter had been breached, and that rifle company was taking "light enemy fire" in their sector. There was a collective groan as a good portion of the crowd got up and collected their things. "Man, are you *kidding me*?" "Come on!" They seemed more annoyed that they would miss the rest of the show than worried about heading into combat.

I understood their mentality, though. These guys were under a lot of pressure to accomplish their missions. When there was an opportunity to stop and take in a show, it made them feel normal again. For a little while they could let go of that fear and anxiety and feel closer to home. The soldiers talked an awful lot about what they would do when they were "back in the world," as if Vietnam were on some distant planet. Our job was to give them a little reminder that the world they wanted to get back to was still there waiting for them. The title of "entertainer" took on a more meaningful aspect in Vietnam.

Thousands of soldiers were out there that night, even after Bravo Company left, and it seemed like every single one wanted to come shake hands after the show. I was trying to shake as many as possible when I recognized a face from back home.

This guy named Theodore Lovett, whom I knew from my childhood in Kinston, fought his way to the front of the crowd just to speak to me. In the midst of all the mayhem, we shook hands and tried to catch up, but it was too crazy out there to really carry on a conversation. He was very worked up and kept telling me how the army wasn't treating the black soldiers right, singling them out for dangerous combat missions more than the white soldiers. He wanted me to get word to someone who could do something about it. I told him I'd do what I could, not knowing what, if anything, I actually could do. We couldn't speak for very long, but we said that we'd see one another "back in the world" once his tour was up. About a year later, on my next extended trip home to Kinston, I learned that Theodore never made it back to the world. He'd been killed in Vietnam not long after I saw him. He was one of several young men from Kinston whom I knew personally who died there, including my classmates James Avent and Johnny Miller, my longtime neighbor from the Carver Court projects, Sylvester Brown, and Charles Whitfield, a trumpet player who had played with my uncle in the Blue Notes. There were others whom I didn't know. The Vietnam War made a big impact on the tiny town of Kinston, and I wondered if there was some truth in what Theodore tried to tell me.

Many of the black leaders, including Martin Luther King Jr., spoke out against the war and criticized the way the government treated its black soldiers. The numbers didn't lie, and black soldiers were being killed in disproportionate numbers. The Vietnam War revealed some very ugly truths about how the government still treated blacks, and out of that arose a new sense of black solidarity.

The year 1968 was a roller coaster of highs and lows for me, but one of the best things that came out of it, and one of the best things that I've been a part of in terms of James Brown's music, was the recording of "Say It Loud, I'm Black and I'm Proud" in August. The song featured a choir of children on the chorus, chanting the incredibly positive refrain, which eventually became part of the national conscience. That song almost overnight took back the word "black" from the people who'd used it for generations as a derogatory term and made it something for us to be proud to say. The chant spread like wildfire and was an instant hit. Before that, to refer to oneself as "black" was almost unheard of. The word had been used as a weapon for so long that it almost felt strange to celebrate it. But the black power movement was in full swing, and this song was its anthem. In October of that year, at the Olympic Games in Mexico City, Tommie Smith and John Carlos gave the now famous black power salute after they won gold and bronze in the 200-meter race. It was a controversial but powerful statement that echoed what an entire nation of repressed people were feeling: we were proud of who we were and wouldn't hide that pride any longer. We weren't negro or colored or anything else. We were *black* and proud of it.

All of this black pride and self-respect didn't mean that James dealt with the members of the band any differently than he always had, unfortunately. Despite the fact that this core group was probably the best band he'd ever had up to that point, his attitude was still, "It's my way or the highway." We were treated with increasing dismissal and, at times, outright disrespect.

Not long after the recording of "Say It Loud" was finished, James's mentor and manager, Ben Bart, died of a heart attack. James and Ben weren't working together at the time, as there had been some argument over money, but I think James took Ben Bart's death really hard. I know that after it happened, he began to take on more responsibility for managing himself.

By this time, James had reached the pinnacle of his success and influence. He'd bought several radio stations, opened a fried chicken franchise, and was actively involved in politics. He was invited to dinner at the White House that year and campaigned for Hubert Humphrey for president. After the show in Boston, politicians realized that James had considerable influence over the black community. Nixon even invited him to play his inaugural ball the following year, which ironically enough ended up costing James a lot of the influence he had with the black community. James's increasing involvement in business and politics began to make him more distant from the band itself and created more work for everyone involved in the day-to-day operations. While the band traveled around in the bus, James would swoop in at the last minute, fresh from his private plane, just before showtime. And since he could come and go as he pleased, more or less, he didn't think twice about conducting pointless rehearsals all night if he wasn't happy about something.

St. Clair wasn't the only musician James had me fire for him—far from it. I was routinely called on to fire musicians when James was unhappy with someone, only to be sent out ahead of the band to the next city to "recruit" musicians for the next night's show.

I can't begin to tell you how difficult it is to find good musicians on short notice, even in a town like St. Louis or Memphis, and it became exhausting after a while.

Around this time, Pee Wee decided that he'd had enough and resigned as bandleader, which then became Fred's job. Fred and I weren't extremely close at the time, but an incident one afternoon during rehearsal solidified our friendship. As the new band director, he'd worked out a new arrangement for a tune we were doing and was rehearsing it with the band. It was a great arrangement, and I discovered a whole new appreciation for Fred, not only as a player but as an arranger as well.

As usual, James came in during the middle of the rehearsal and stopped everything. He began yelling at Fred, telling him his new arrangement was crap and not at all what he wanted. He grabbed charts off the music stands and ripped them up in Fred's face, telling him that he was going to be fired as bandleader.

It was erratic behavior, even for James, and I knew that Fred didn't deserve any of the verbal abuse he was getting. I stepped in and told James what I thought.

"Mr. Brown, I think Mr. Wesley is doing a fantastic job, and I really like his arrangements."

Offering up my own observation did not go over well at all. James didn't like to have anything he said contradicted by anyone in his employ, least of all in front of the entire band like that. He just looked at me like I was crazy and went on berating Fred, calling him a "half-soldier" at one point. I have no idea what that meant, but the fallout from the incident came soon after with Fred's departure from the band.

By the spring of 1970, my patience was wearing thin with James and his treatment of the band. The morale was at an all-time low because of our erratic touring schedule and lack of proper payment. The fact that my duties had increased considerably and my pay had not meant that I was nearing the end of my rope. I wondered if it was time to give my dream of having my own band a shot but also considered the possibility of joining someone else's band. Whatever the next step was, I realized that it was time to move on. As it turned out, I wasn't the only one with that thought.

7

All the King's Men

By the end of 1970, Pee Wee and Fred had left James's band, and I really wanted to take a break. I was worn out from the endless traveling, the pointless rehearsals, the rules and the fines—all of it. Mostly I was tired of not getting the compensation I deserved. I felt like my solos on recordings like "Papa's Got a Brand New Bag" and "Cold Sweat" really elevated those songs and helped make them hits. But going to James and asking for more money felt like begging to me, and I never did that. What I wanted more than the money was the recognition that my talent was worth something and for James to compensate me of his own accord. I had waited around for years, and it was clear that wasn't going to happen. As I pondered leaving the band I remembered a piece of advice that James had given me years ago in one of those moments he dropped his defenses and was really honest. He told me that I should never let my name get buried in another name. Now the name "Maceo" was getting buried under James Brown's name. I'd always wanted to have my own group, and I knew that it would never happen as long as I was part of his band.

I've always felt confident. I never intended to be a sideman forever, and playing with James Brown's band was in many ways a stepping-stone to something larger. I looked at it like a train ride: there were stops along the way between points *A* and *Z*, and it would have been nice if the train rolled straight through, but this train zigged and zagged all over the place. If you didn't like where the train was headed you were free to get off at any time, and, for me, it was that time.

I decided I wanted it documented that I was *leaving* and not being fired. James had fired so many musicians over the years that I wanted it clear that my decision to leave was exactly that—*my* decision. I wanted to make that statement loud and clear. I mentioned this to Melvin and some of the other guys in the band one night, and it really sparked a fire. They were already unhappy about the payroll situation (among other things), and morale was at an all-time low. One thing that came up in conversation was the fact that I was wearing so many different hats—emcee, comedian, and soloist—and was still only paid the regular wage like everyone else. If I wasn't treated fairly, how could they expect to be?

Soon I wasn't the only one in the band talking about leaving. An idea surfaced: to all leave together and form our own band. We already had the chemistry and plenty of tunes we could perform. And what performer wouldn't jump at the chance to have James Brown's band behind them? What we were talking about was unheard of in James's band, because groupthink was very much discouraged. In many ways, James worked to divide and conquer the band, probably to avoid that sort of mutiny.

No matter how bad things were, leaving the band was still a big risk. We weren't paid badly, but it was never enough to give us the security to plan farther ahead than the next gig. The idea of the entire band walking out started to sound like a real possibility, but first we wondered if we should give James the opportunity to sweeten the pot. Richard Griffith, who was called Kush, finally came up with an ultimatum. Either James would pay the band more and pay me for all the extra duties I'd taken on, or the band would leave. Period. To be successful, the plan required an act of solidarity on the part of everyone in the band, and although I was still set on leaving on my own, I eventually relented and agreed to stand with the band.

After our next show in Jacksonville, Florida, we presented James with our list of grievances. Either our demands for better pay and better treatment would be met by a certain time, or he would be without a band. As it turned out, James had no intention of giving in to our demands. Instead he secretly dialed up Bootsy Collins and his brother Phelps ("Catfish") and had them bring their band down from Cincinnati to play the next show in Florida. I found out from Bootsy years later that his band was under the impression they were coming down to play *with us*, not replace us. I don't know if they would have refused even if they knew the truth, but I believe they went down there with the best of intentions. Somehow James also talked Fred into coming back because he needed someone to get the new band in shape and teach them all the music. We were unaware that any of this was going on and received word just before the deadline that there would be no change in policy. We knew what we had to do. Remaining true to our word, we made the announcement that we were all leaving the band.

James may have been prepared for our walking out like that, but our departure caused a big ruckus with everyone else. That evening, the phones in the hotel were ringing off the hook, and people were running around everywhere trying to figure out what to do. As I walked by one room I overheard the road manager, Jimmy Smith, on the phone telling someone what was going on.

"They all left," he yelled into the receiver. Whoever was on the end obviously didn't grasp the situation. "*Everyone*," Jimmy yelled.

"I'm telling you, all of the king's horses and all the king's men. They all left!"

I heard that, and I knew instantly that Maceo and All the King's Men had to be the name of our new band.

So much has been said over the years about our departure it's hard to sort out the fact from the fiction. I can tell you that we left things in a very businesslike fashion. We gave James an ultimatum that he did not accept, so we kept our word and left—end of story. There wasn't a great deal of animosity or name-calling, which is how the situation has been described in some interviews I've read.

Starting our own group was exciting in the beginning. The band consisted of me and Eldee Williams on saxophone, Melvin on drums, Kush and Joe Davis on trumpet, Jimmy Nolen and Alfonzo Kellum on guitar, and Bernard Odum on bass. We were all really young and didn't have the kind of serious responsibilities that would have kept us from taking a chance on this new band. We all recognized the risk involved, but with youth comes a sense of invincibility, and we were ready to roll the dice.

At first, we were based out of Louisville, Kentucky, because Kush's family lived there and his father had a network of places for the band to stay rent-free. This living arrangement was too good to pass up, because we needed to save all the money we could to get everything off the ground. When we arrived Kush's father arranged a small gig for us so his friends could come and check us out. Everyone was really friendly and supportive, and after the gig they began offering us rooms in their homes. It was a little like being picked for a game of football at recess, but we were grateful for the help. We knew once we had our living arrangements taken care of we could start planning our next move.

No one in the band really had much experience with the business side of things, so we had to find someone to manage us. Joe was from Nashville and had some connections with Lelan Rogers, Kenny Rogers's brother, who had a small record label there and expressed an interest in recording and managing the band. I wasn't convinced that this particular management deal was the best move for us, since Lelan seemed to be more in touch with country and western music, but it was decided that a bad deal was better than no deal at all. We signed with House of Fox Records and made the trip down to Nashville to record our first record, *Doing Their Own Thing*. The title really summed up the motto of the band. In the studio, the band's natural chemistry came out, and we let that guide us. Kush wrote out the arrangements and we all took solos on the songs we thought we could play the best on. The last track on *Doing Their Own Thing* was titled "I Remember Mr. Banks" and was a tribute to my high school band director and mentor. I thought about Banks often and knew how proud he would have been to see my name on the cover of a record.

The King's Men adopted a system of majority rule that worked out well for a while. Because we'd been under James's thumb for so long, this democratic system was really appealing. Coming from a situation where everything was dictated to us, from the clothes we wore onstage to who would play a solo on what song, it felt good to be in control and involved in decisions. When it came time to book gigs, everyone came to the table with ideas about clubs they were familiar with, how much money we could make there, and where we could stay. When we were paid after a gig we reimbursed everyone for their expenses, and the rest was split equally. If someone needed travel money because they pitched in for gas or had to drive a long way, they were reimbursed for that. It didn't take long to see that, after expenses, there wasn't really much money to go around. But for us it wasn't about the money. There was a certain pride in defying James Brown.

That defiance came with a price, though. James wasn't happy about our departure and was even less happy that we'd formed a new band. He saw himself as a businessman, and to him the King's Men were competition; like any businessman, he worked to wipe out the opposition. We tried to promote ourselves with what money we had, but we were no match for James's wealth and influence. When we took our record to the disc jockeys at radio stations we were often told that they'd been paid not to play it. We would show up in a city for a gig and find all of our posters had been mysteriously torn down. Sometimes we'd get onstage to find that there were only three or four people in the audience. Once we played in Augusta, and the only one there was James's daddy, who really liked the King's Men. He knew what his son had done, why there wasn't anyone at the club, and just shook his head. "J-J-J-Junior is *crazy*," he said through his stutter.

This sort of sabotage became a regular occurrence. There were times when James gave another group that was playing in town on the same night money to promote their show, which, given our limited budget, was more than we could compete with. His antics weren't a giant secret; they came as no surprise to us when we learned of them. We kept in touch with some of the people in his organization, and more than once we heard that James had made comments that suggested he knew our record wasn't going to get played anywhere. He had quite a bit of influence with disc jockeys and promoters and wasn't above leaning on these people to get his way. The things James did to derail our band really angered some of the guys in the band, but I never took it personally. James Brown could do whatever he wanted, but I was still going to be Maceo Parker and could play like nobody else. He couldn't take that from me no matter what he did.

Aside from our own gigs we hired ourselves out as a backing band for singers like Jean Knight ("Mr. Big Stuff") and Johnnie Taylor ("Who's Making Love"). We always had a lot of fun with Johnnie, who had a great presence onstage—the ladies really ate up what he put out. Despite all the frustrations, we tore it up and wore people *out*. A gentleman came up to me after one show and told me that we were the best band he'd seen since James Brown. I had to laugh at that. We didn't have the red carpet rolled out for us like we were used to, but we made it work for a while.

There wasn't a bus anymore, but we would often rent a small van or caravan in several cars. One afternoon on the way to a gig our cramped van crested a hill only to find a car parked right in our lane. Levi Raspberry happened to be driving and instantly jerked the wheel to avoid hitting the car. As the van fishtailed out of control and left the road, I grabbed Melvin around the neck and held on for dear life. It happened in the blink of an eye, but in those situations time seems to slow to a crawl. Everyone was yelling and shouting as the van bumped along over the grassy median heading straight toward some oncoming traffic. Just then I noticed the trailer full of our gear that we were pulling had come loose and was passing the van on the right side. If things weren't so terrifying, that might have been funny. As we hit the oncoming lanes, the traffic zoomed past and the van and trailer just ahead of it skirted right through a break in the cars. I started to breathe a sigh of relief when I noticed we were headed directly for a lake with only a giant tree directly in our path to keep us from going underwater. By the grace of God the van and trailer both rumbled to a halt before hitting the tree, and I finally let go of poor Melvin's neck. We were all very lucky to be alive. Mother always prayed for our safety while out on the road, and I knew her prayers kept us safe that afternoon. Luckily none of the equipment was damaged and we made it to the gig, but it shook everyone up a bit and exposed some frayed nerves.

Maceo and All the King's Men held it together for about a year before the strain and stress of it all really got to everyone. We were out on the road with no support from our label and doing everything for ourselves. In the beginning, it seemed that Lelan was going to be a good manager and treat us fairly, but once the albums were recorded, we hardly ever heard from him again. When the albums were released we were horrified to discover that the producers had added all kinds of strings to the tracks, choking off all the funk we'd put in. Between James's efforts to stifle our records and House of Fox's lackluster marketing efforts, we never saw a dime from those recordings.

Our bad management was starting to put a strain on things, and eventually our system of democratic rule broke down. What started out as a way to involve everyone in the business of the band had become a system of equalizing things musically. Discussions about how many choruses someone had on a particular song or how many songs someone was singing became more and more frequent. It didn't matter who could sing better or who played better solos, spreading the limelight around became a big issue. This sort of bickering shouldn't have been surprising, given that we were all essentially sidemen who were enjoying our first bit of notoriety. But it began to cause a lot of friction between guys who had been great friends for years. It got to the point where people stopped asking to be reimbursed for their expenses and just started taking the money without consulting the group. It was very hard to watch, but I could see where things were headed.

The situation in the band finally spiraled so far out of balance that I had to get away. I was feeling like I needed a break, not just from the band, but from the music business altogether. I was twenty-nine years old and had been playing continuously for nearly two decades. In 1971, I called it quits with the King's Men, packed up my things, and headed home to be with Carolyn and the kids in Brooklyn.

Carolyn's family lived in a small two-story brick building right on the corner of Saratoga and Sumpter in Bedford Stuyvesant, the center of the black universe in Brooklyn. None of the houses in the neighborhood had yards the way they did in Kinston, so the people hung out on the stoops in front of their doors, and I got to know some of them. Adjusting to being home 100 percent of the time was just like adjusting to dorm life or life on the road: it was a routine I had to get used to. I had to learn where to shop for meat and fresh vegetables, how long the supermarket stayed open, where the dry-cleaning place was. It seemed like there were candy stores everywhere, and I'd pick up treats for the kids on the way home sometimes. Sumpter Street was a one-way street with alternate parking. For a few days a week, everyone parked on one side and then had to move to the other side so the street sweeper could get through. It was funny to me that once I had to remember to shine my shoes and get my suits pressed or risk being fined by James Brown, and now I had to remember to move the car regularly or risk getting a parking ticket from the city.

My father-in-law, Bill, had a rubbish-removal business at the time and gave me a job with him for a while. (Years later I recorded "Blues for Shorty Bill" as a tribute to him.) When I had been on the road and come through, Bill used to joke that he knew I was in town because when he came home something special was in the kitchen. "Maceo must be in town because my wife is cooking," he would joke. Now, though, I was there permanently and things were different.

Instead of killing onstage, my days were spent killing myself hauling heavy loads of debris away from construction sites. It wasn't glamorous work, but I found that I actually enjoyed it. The other guys were all really funny, and we'd spend our days laughing and cutting up to break the monotony of the job. James had a song called "Greedy Man" in which he would shout, "Pick up on this," and that became our battle cry at work. When we had to lift heavy pieces of an old boiler or a pile of sheet rock into the dump truck I would shout out, "Pick up on this!" It was cool and made everyone laugh.

We had a lot of fun, even though it was exhausting work that required some skill and know-how. It wasn't like you could just dump all of this heavy stuff in the back of the dump truck and go. Things had to be spread around so when the back was elevated to dump everything out at the end of the day, all the debris didn't bunch up in the middle and cause a blockage. I learned how to load the truck and how to carry the heavy pails on my shoulders so I didn't strain my back. It wasn't what I was used to, but it felt OK to be away from the saxophone and good to be doing something new.

One afternoon we had to go underneath this building that was under renovation to remove all the construction materials that had accumulated there. We spent the entire day crawling around in the dust and dirt, hauling out buckets full of old bricks and lengths of pipe. I emerged from under the building covered with grime with a bucket of bricks on my shoulder and came face to face with Chuck Fowler, the piano player from my army band back in Bremerhaven, Germany. I stood there for a minute thinking about all the times I'd talked about getting out of the army and going back to work for James Brown. How was I going to explain that I wasn't really working with him right now? Chuck and I talked for a bit, and I told him I was "helping my father-in-law out for a while." For the first time, though, I thought about putting down my bucket and picking up the saxophone again.

It must have seemed strange that I'd gone from such a high-profile job in the music business to hauling around trash, but I didn't see it that way. Playing the saxophone was like a safety net to me; it was always there when I needed to fall back on it. Rubbish removal paid twenty-five to thirty dollars a day, which was not the kind of money I was accustomed to, but I didn't worry about that. I needed to be away from show business for a while, and I was accomplishing what I wanted to do at the time. I knew this break was temporary, and when I was ready to pick up the horn again and look for a serious gig, I would. I also knew if I decided to go back to work with James, I could. I looked at the James Brown Band as an institution of higher learning: it was always going to be there, and I could go back if and when I was ready. I was Maceo Parker whether I was hauling bricks in overalls and a hard hat or playing onstage at the Apollo in a tuxedo.

I'd been in New York for several months when I found out that James was doing a show in Brooklyn. It had been more than a year since I'd seen anyone in the band, and I thought I'd just stop in and say hello. I had no intention of going back, but I'd had enough of a break to start toying with the idea of playing again. I knew how James could really carry a grudge for a while, and part of me wanted to test the waters.

I walked down to the club the night of the gig and got within earshot of the bus when I heard an all-too-familiar voice. Gertrude was upset and yelling at someone in the band, saying, "You know *good and well* Mr. Brown isn't gonna like you doing that!"

That was enough for me. I didn't stick around to hear the rest and just turned around and went home without saying a word to anyone. It was too soon.

I continued to work at the rubbish-removal business for the rest of the year, rarely touching my horn. By the winter of 1972, I had been away from performing for more than a year. Construction work, especially up north, tends to drop off during the winter months, which meant I was working less and consequently short on money occasionally. During the weeks when things got a little scarce, I noticed how some of the guys would come to my father-in-law and ask him for an advance on their next paycheck. The concept of an advance on your wages was something new to me. In the army we were paid regularly, and in James's band we were paid cash nightly (most of the time). There was no such thing as an "advance" on the next night's show. The holidays were coming up, and I needed a little extra money, so I asked for "one of those advances" I'd seen the other guys getting.

Bill just looked at me and asked, "What do *you* need money for?"

I may not have been ready to get back on the road, but I knew right then it was time for me to leave the blue-collar world behind.

As luck would have it, a few weeks later I bumped into Pee Wee, who was in New York City doing some studio work with Esther Phillips on her album *Alone Again, Naturally*. He mentioned that the producer, Creed Taylor, needed a tenor player for a few of the sessions and asked me if I was interested in some work. It was two or three weeks before Christmas and I needed the extra money, so I accepted.

Pee Wee and Creed brought together some amazing session players for that album, including Ron Carter and George Benson, and I was a little nervous at first since I was really rusty. I have to admit I didn't do such a great job on that recording, but what I played was good enough to make the session and get paid. I knew it was time to get serious about playing again; that's what I was meant to do.

James was also in New York at that time working on his new record label, People Records, so it was convenient to get in touch with him. People was part of a giant deal he'd recently signed with Polydor Records in which he was required to produce several full albums a year for himself and several other artists he managed. It was a bold move because, until then, James had mainly focused on an endless stream of singles. The label was populated with people from James's inner circle, like Lyn Collins, Hank Ballard, Bobby Byrd, and Fred Wesley—a stable of artists he called "the First Family of Soul."

I was excited about the new record label because it seemed like an opportunity for me to finally explore the concept I'd had for years of working with my own group. Fred was working as James's bandleader and had already cut a few records with a group called the J.B.'s. The sound of James's music had changed since I'd been away, with the emphasis shifting from the horn section to the rhythm section. But now that Fred was back and writing arrangements, the funky horns were front and center again.

The first recording I worked on as part of the family was "Doing It to Death," which people often call "Gonna Have a Funky Good Time" because of the refrain that is repeated over and over again. Before the session, James made the suggestion that I play the alto saxophone instead of the tenor.

"You play really funky on the tenor," he told me, "but I don't know too many people playing like that on the *little* horn."

That's what James called the alto, the "little horn." I trusted his instincts because he had been right about so many things musically.

James liked to keep things loose in the studio and often recorded a lot of spontaneous dialogue instead of actual lyrics. When we started the recording for "Doing It to Death," James started rapping to the band and mentioned that someone important was back but played around and wouldn't call my name right away.

"In a minute, I'm gonna call that brother with the little horn, but I don't want to say his name just yet."

After a few choruses and Fred's trombone solo, James called out to Fred.

"Who's that over there?"

"I think that's Maceo," Fred responded.

"Who?"

"Maceo. You know, like, 'Maceo, won't you blow,'" Fred shouted.

"Oh yeah, Maceo!" James sounded ecstatic. "Are you back, brother?"

For some reason I didn't want to say officially on record that I was back, so I just fumbled for a second and eventually replied with something like, "Sounds real good in here." James wasn't satisfied, though.

"Yeah, but are you *back*, brother?" James asked.

He wanted to know if I was there to stay. I just smiled at him and took a solo rather than answering. I was back, but I figured I'd let my playing do the talking. After a bit James nodded to the flute sitting in the corner. I took the saxophone off my neck and started raising the microphone when James motioned to me to come over to his microphone and play, but I just got on my knees and played a flute solo right there. James just laughed and carried on like it was the best thing he'd ever seen.

It was a great session that really captured that particular moment. We were together and having fun again, and that feeling really came across. "Doing It to Death" was huge that summer and became a number one hit for Fred and the J.B.'s.

It was really good to see my old friends like Fred and a few of the King's Men like Jimmy Nolen and Eldee Williams who had returned to the band as well. It might seem strange that so many musicians could just come and go in the James Brown organization, especially given the way some people left the band, but James regarded the musicians in the band as chess pieces. Sometimes he would lose a few pieces and sometimes he'd win a few back, but he just made do with the pieces he had at the time and the game went on. The band was a revolving door in that sense; you left when you wanted to and came back when you were ready. In the band, we had a saying. When you were ready to rejoin the band, you strolled in and announced, "I'm back," and everything was cool. James had two important pieces back on the board with Fred and me.

During my first show back with the band I was introduced to Lyn Collins. Lyn had recorded an album called *Think* that James produced, but she would sing whatever was hot at the time, material that James selected for her—Aretha Franklin or Etta James tunes—during the show. Lyn was very beautiful, and I remember standing beside Fred at the end of the stage and catching a glimpse of her walking onto the stage out of the corner of my eye. Right in the middle of the show I yelled out, "Whoa!" which got a huge laugh from the crowd and embarrassed Lyn a little. Later Fred pulled me aside and let me know that I couldn't do stuff like that. I was just being silly, but he was right. I was lucky I wasn't fined for that.

I could never figure out why, but James treated Lyn really harshly. He used to tell her right before the show that he wanted her to do a new tune that she wasn't familiar with. She had to scramble around to find a recording of the song to learn the lyrics, which wasn't always possible. After seeing him do this to her a few times, I started writing out lyrics to help her rehearse the song for the show. She was incredibly grateful to me, which was the basis for our eventual friendship.

I was really excited about performing on the big stage again, and James was equally excited about having me back. The prodigal son had returned, and I was embraced by the man himself, so much so that James kept me close for a time, traveling with him personally. I decided I needed to step up my dress and go with a three-piece suit instead of the usual two-piece. We had always dressed nicely in the band, but when you were traveling as part of James's personal entourage, you had to go the extra mile. The way James embraced me when I came back reminded me of the way he'd been with Melvin in '64 when we joined the band. It seemed like my stock had gone up since my departure, and I began to feel a sense of pride in being part of his band that I hadn't felt since the early days.

As part of the First Family of Soul I was given the opportunity to record an album, and almost immediately after my return we started work on *Us*, the first album from Maceo and the Macks. James thought up the name, probably inspired by the film *The Mack*. My group was essentially James's band with me out in front, which wasn't exactly what I had in mind. I would have preferred to select my own musicians, but I quickly realized that decision wasn't up to me.

James also picked out the tunes for the session, which included instrumental versions of songs that were hot at the time and a reworking of his song "It's a Man's Man's Man's World" as "Soul of a Black Man." Fred wrote the arrangements out and produced everything, with James standing over his shoulder most of the time. I don't know why I expected James to come to me and ask me to write a few tunes for the album. Even though I'd written songs and would have been glad to come up with some original material for *my* album, I didn't assert myself and suggest any of them because I'd seen the way he shot down things that Fred came up with from time to time. Fred had some great ideas for songs that everyone in the band really loved, but James would flat-out tell him they were crappy and belittle him in front of his troupe of yes-men. I wasn't going to put myself through that.

I'd written a song for Maceo and All the King's Men called "Got to Get'cha," inspired by a poem that my brother Kellis had written. I came up with the groove, and the hook was something I'd heard James say one time during a show, but the lyrics came nearly verbatim from Kellis's poem:

> I need a bottle of scotch, for all the love I've got.
> I need a Cupid's arrow, shoot it straight and narrow.
> I need a chicken leg, just to make her beg.
> I got to get'cha, I got to get'cha.

James later told me that I might have had a hit with that song if I hadn't used the word "scotch." When I wrote the lyric I thought it would be all right because Ray Charles had a hit with "Let's Go Get Stoned," where he mentions getting a bottle of gin, but James was convinced that the mention of alcohol was the reason the song never took off. I wasn't sure that he was right, considering all the work he'd done to bury that album.

I was really disappointed when *Us* came out with my name and face on the cover but hardly any of *me* inside. I may have played all over it, but I knew it was really just another James Brown record. I hadn't been back very long but was already beginning to see that this new record label wasn't as much about producing new artists as it was about creating new revenue streams for James Brown.

Us never really took off, although "Soul of a Black Man" became really popular as the B-side to the Maceo and the Macks single "Cross the Track (We Better Go Back)," which came out in the fall of 1974. Fred had said to me that James wanted us to record a song based on an idea James had thought up. As usual, James had a rough idea of what the song should sound like and had hummed and grunted the melody to Fred, and the "lyrics" had something to do with the phrase "across the tracks." I thought for a minute and tried to think like James would. "Across the tracks" was a metaphor for the ghetto or the wrong side of town; I knew that James had come out of the ghetto and had no intention of ever going back. Still, I thought it would be an interesting idea for him to go back and see what was going on there. In many ways, James's political ideas had isolated him from the people across the tracks and he was a bit out of touch with that world. I was thinking out loud and said, "You ought to get right back. Tell me what it's like, across the tracks," and that was it. We had the hook for the song.

Vicki Anderson did the female vocal parts in sort of a call-and-response motif: "I *live* across the tracks and I *know* what it's like." It was hot. James added this little octave part on the Farfisa (a tiny electric organ) that sounded like a siren going off. I thought it was unnecessary and a little out of tune, but we'd learned to let things like that alone. We used to laugh all the time because James could be really out, but later we'd see that the funny ideas he had in the studio would often become the thing that made the song a big hit. He had great instincts that way.

"Soul Power '74" was another great recording from this period. It was originally a tune James recorded as "Soul Power" when Bootsy was in the band. James had the idea to take his vocals off and rerecord it as an instrumental with a new horn melody. After it was recorded some funny sound effects were added along with a bit of Martin Luther King Jr.'s "I've Been to the Mountaintop" speech. That record was a big hit in 1974 and has become one of the most sampled bits of music in pop and hip-hop.

Despite my disappointment over the *Us* album, those were really fun times because the pride was still there in the band. There was a real sense of unity in the group that hadn't been there before. We were the First Family of Soul, and we really felt like a family. One family member was Lee Austin, James's longtime friend from Augusta. He was crazy. His nickname was "the Burner" because he would do all these wild cartwheels onstage and just burn the thing down. Lee originally traveled around with the band as James's hairdresser for many years, but he really wanted to be a singer and constantly pestered James to give him a shot at recording. Eventually James relented and brought us all into the studio to record Little Richard's "Tutti Frutti."

Now, as much fun as everyone had clowning around backstage and on the road, the studio was a different matter because James was paying for the studio time and really wanted everyone to be serious. "Tutti Frutti" is a famous song, and everyone knows how the song starts out: "Wop bopaloobop, a wop bam boom!" For some reason, though, Lee couldn't get that line down. We started the first take and Lee messed up, so James waved his arms and stopped everything. He just cocked his head to the side and looked at Lee in disbelief.

"What did you say?" he asked. "That's not the way it goes. Try it again."

We tried the intro several more times and it just wasn't coming out right, so James stopped the band again. Lee was getting a little flustered, and James was obviously getting irritated. I wanted to laugh, but you were supposed to be serious when you were in the studio, so I just held it in.

After a few more tries, it was obvious that Lee just wasn't getting it the way James wanted to hear it and James was running out of ideas to get things on the right track.

Finally, overcome with frustration, James yelled out, "Fred! Write that out on a piece of paper for him."

That's when it got really funny.

Like any good bandleader, Fred got out a magic marker and started to write out the words on cue cards. I wanted to laugh so badly it hurt. After a second, Fred looked up at me with a confused look on his face.

"Hey, Maceo. How do you spell 'bopaloobop'?"

I just lost it. I wanted to be serious, but the situation was just too ludicrous. Eventually we regained our composure and tried the thing again, this time with "Wop bopaloobop" written out on one cue card and "a wop bam boom!" on another. James had someone stand in front of the vocal microphone and hold the cards up so Lee could read them. I felt bad for him, but the whole situation was just too funny not to laugh.

Finally he got the line down and we moved on to the rest of the song, but by then Lee had become a little strained from singing the intro so many times, and in the middle of a verse his voice went out. James just lost it.

"Didn't you ask me to give you a chance?" he yelled. "Didn't you ask me to record you? Well I'm giving you a chance."

All Lee could do was ask for some water in a raspy whisper. We weren't supposed to be laughing, but I couldn't help it. I was crying. James finally had enough and just sent everyone home for the day.

Aside from all of the recording we were doing, we did a lot of television appearances as well. All the extra exposure was getting my name out there, and about that time I found out that offers were coming in to Jack Bart's booking office from promoters for me to do solo shows. I overheard someone talking about it one day, and it really got the wheels turning in my head. I approached James about the situation and let him know I was interested in putting something together for these gigs. I knew I could play whatever was hot at the time as well as the new songs we'd recorded like "Soul Power '74." Then there were always the James Brown standards like "Try Me" that I could fall back on. It would also be a great opportunity for me to sing a little, something I'd done with James's band from time to time.

We discussed it and eventually James decided that he would let me go out on my own and play some of the shows. The only catch was I had to give him a percentage of what I made: 15 percent went to Jack Bart at Universal Entertainment for the bookings, and 10 percent went to James himself. Why he felt entitled to a percentage of my earnings, I'm not sure. Maybe it was just for the privilege of being allowed to go out on my own. It wasn't an ideal situation, but the opportunity to finally explore my concept with my own band was too good to pass up. I knew some cats in Brooklyn I could get together, and I'd seen another really solid band in Philadelphia called the Glass Menagerie that I thought I could work with. I rehearsed each group and before long was out on the weekends playing everywhere from street festivals to clubs.

I think James knew how badly I wanted to have my own band, and perhaps he saw this bit of independence as a concession to keep me around a little longer. To my knowledge he never let anyone else go out and gig on their own. This period was a really important time for me as an artist because I developed my stage presence and showmanship. I was free to explore my ideas and had fun developing what I thought was an entertaining set.

I worked out one idea where just before the set break I would get deep into a solo and have the band walk off one by one, leaving only the drummer. To the crowd it was supposed to look as if I was so into what I was doing that I didn't notice that the band had left. I'd turn around and act shocked to see an empty stage; then I'd make my way over to the piano to do a solo ballad. I'd always liked singing, and this was a way for me to showcase another side that I rarely got the opportunity to explore onstage. I had been discouraged from singing before because I'd been told I sounded like Ray Charles, which I never understood. Still, audiences really liked it when I sang like Ray, so at this point in the set I'd sit at the piano and do a tune like "Georgia" and really get into it. Afterward the band would come back onstage and we'd play a swing number with me still behind the piano. Another thing I started doing at this time was walking out into the crowd during a solo and mingling with the people. There's a certain risk in leaving the stage like that, because it takes away from the mystique of the performer and makes you more accessible to the audience, but I found I liked connecting with the crowd, a concept that I brought back with me to James's band.

All the recording and playing extra shows meant I was making more money and could move my family from the house on Sumpter Street to a small apartment on Saratoga around the corner. We stayed there about a year and worked on renovating the place with new paneling on the walls and new plumbing. It wasn't too long after all the renovation was completed, though, that we decided to move the family down to Kinston. As nice as the apartment was, I started to realize I wasn't comfortable with the neighborhood and the pace of life in Brooklyn. When the kids were babies what was happening on the street didn't matter as much, but they were getting older, starting to ask questions about all the pimps and winos who hung around on the corner, and I didn't like that. I was used to the South, where things moved a little more slowly, and realized that Kinston was a better environment for my kids to grow up in. Carolyn and the kids stayed with my mother for a time while I was constantly in between recording sessions, gigs with James, and my own commitments with my band.

As 1974 drew to a close, I felt like things were going well for me. My life was certainly much more hectic than it had been when I was hauling rubbish a few years earlier, but then again, things were tumultuous everywhere in the country. The war in Vietnam was still dragging on, Nixon had just resigned over the Watergate scandal, and drugs were destroying inner-city neighborhoods. The civil rights movement of the 1960s had birthed a new black consciousness in the nation that was reflected in everything from politics to fashion—and especially music. Hank Aaron shattered Babe Ruth's home-run record that year, which I was excited to see, even though I was (and still am) a die-hard Yankees fan. Everywhere you looked, black culture was at the forefront of the American experience.

No single event in 1974 better personified this new black consciousness than the Ali vs. Foreman fight in Kinshasa, Zaire, the famous "Rumble in the Jungle." Don King, the promoter, wanted to put together an all-star music festival to coincide with the monumental fight, and James had signed on to headline the show. In September, I packed my bags and boarded the private plane with the band and some of the other artists on the bill. We were about to witness one of the greatest moments not only in sports but in American history.

8

Take a Ride on the Mothership

It's hard to put into words the kind of hype that surrounded the Rumble in the Jungle. I don't think any sporting event has ever come close to creating the kind of spectacle that fight produced. George Foreman was in his prime then, a complete wrecking ball of a man, and Muhammad Ali, already a legend, was looking to regain the heavyweight title after his suspension for refusing the draft. The press conferences produced some of the most well-known Ali quotes, and Don King capitalized on the black power movement of the time. It was a dramatic fight that saw Ali's now-famous "rope-a-dope" defense that wore down Foreman and allowed Ali to knock him out in the eighth round.

James Brown was scheduled to headline the giant concert that was to accompany the fight, along with a list of top-notch performers like B.B. King, Bill Withers, and the Spinners, among others. I was very happy to meet one performer in particular: Lloyd Price. At one time Lloyd had hired my high school band director and mentor, James Banks, and it was great to reminisce with Lloyd about him.

A delay to the fight caused some chaos surrounding the concert itself, but eventually it all went off as planned. It's hard to recall everything, but one of my clearest memories was watching some people who'd pushed their way through a barricade being dragged away and beaten by the police. Returning to Africa once again had filled me with a sense of black pride, the same feeling I'd felt when I first came there with James's band in 1971, but watching that reminded me of the ugly, shameful side to this place.

After the band returned home, people began leaving, and the entire dynamic shifted again. Things became very stripped down; James stopped the concept of the Flames and even scaled back to just one go-go dancer onstage. Tensions between Fred and James escalated to the point at which Fred decided to leave again, and I completely understood how he felt. I was disenchanted with the whole First Family of Soul concept as well and saw it for what it was: just another money-making venture for James Brown. Eventually Fred hooked up with George Clinton and Bootsy Collins as a horn arranger for several projects, including Bootsy's Rubber Band and Funkadelic, who had become pretty successful.

Now, Fred is a gifted arranger and can really, *really* play some jazz. He knows music theory like he knows his own name, so this kind of space-age funk was a bit of a departure for him, you could say. Fred said in an interview once that he asked George what kind of arrangements he wanted and George just looked at him and said, "Something *baaaaad!*" It was the musical equivalent of the Odd Couple.

I was still with James but unhappy and looking to move on. At the very least, I needed a break. Carolyn and I had three children by this time, and I felt like I wanted to be home, but before I'd really made up my mind about what to do, an offer came that sounded too good to be true. Fred, Bootsy, and George were discussing starting a record label, and they wanted me to get in on the ground floor. I thought to myself, *George, Bootsy, Fred, and me—we can get a lot done with that foursome.* I promptly quit James's band again and made plans to meet Fred in Detroit.

Before the record company idea could materialize, though, George had to fulfill several other recording commitments, so I was brought into the studio to help out. He and Bootsy had recorded a bunch of rhythm tracks but needed Fred's horn parts to fill everything out. I hooked back up with Fred at United Sound in Detroit and started work recording the horn parts he'd arranged for four horns—me on saxophone, Fred on trombone, and two trumpet players, Maurice Davis and Marcus Belgrave. Over the next several months we recorded parts for upcoming records like *Stretchin' Out in Bootsy's Rubber Band, The Mothership Connection,* and *Let's Take It to the Stage.* We recorded along to rhythm tracks that were in various degrees of completeness, so Fred was often putting things together on the fly.

In between all of the recording, we did gigs occasionally with just George at first, and as things progressed eventually we were brought in to play full-time with both Bootsy's band and Funkadelic, which eventually became Parliament-Funkadelic, or P-Funk. Creatively speaking, the music—the *funk*—was all there. Fred brought the horn thing in, solidified the sound, and really made something out of it. The shows, though, were absolute mayhem. If I made any contribution to P-Funk outside of my music, it was some organization.

Let me back up a second by saying that I knew what I was getting myself into. I'd seen George at the Apollo several years before, and the only thing I really remember about the show was thinking to myself that he was absolutely *crazy.* During the chorus of "Loose Booty" he'd turn his butt around to the audience and a spotlight would shine on it. When my friends and I saw that, we fell out laughing. This guy was too silly. I never would have thought in a million years that I'd actually be part of his band one day. But once I found myself onstage with him, I discovered that his theatrics had gotten worse (or better, depending on your perspective).

The first thing I had to get my mind around was the lyrics. Some of them, like "Ga ga goo ga, ga ga goo gaga!" were just nonsense. I had no idea what they meant, and I still don't. They were fun, though. Other lyrics were graphic and blatantly sexual; it took me a long time—a *real* long time—to become comfortable with that stuff. I've said it before and I'll say it again, but my mother brought us up to be "good boys." She'd been to see Melvin and me play with James Brown over the years, but there was no way I wanted her to see me onstage with a man yelling about how he wanted to "tear the roof off the motherfucker."

The clothes these guys wore onstage were another thing. I'd spent the last ten years of my life, off and on, playing with a man who demanded that everyone have a pressed tuxedo and neatly shined shoes before he even looked at the stage. I insist upon sharp dress for my own band to this day—I expect everyone to look like a professional. I tell anyone who plays with me to look like a musician and not like they'd just come back from playing basketball in the park. In George's world, that wasn't a problem. He used to have a giant trunk backstage filled with all kinds of props and costumes, and the band would rummage through it before the gig to pick out what they would wear. A guy would come up to George and say, "Hey, George. I'm really into trains and I was thinking of wearing a conductor's hat and some overalls." George would say, "Cool." If you wanted to dress like an Indian, that was cool, too. A diaper, a sheet, a spaceman outfit—all of that was fine.

One time George's costume didn't arrive in time for the gig, and someone ran in just before showtime to tell him the bad news. George didn't get upset. Instead he just asked around for a spare wig and some boots, then yanked a tablecloth off of the table, wrapped it around himself, and headed out to the stage. He didn't get hung up on the formality of it all. At first, I couldn't believe it. It was fun, it was funky, but it wasn't *me*. Most nights I went with some bell-bottoms, a jacket, and a denim cap and called it a day. My dress was, by the band's standards, extremely conservative. George didn't care what you wore, though. His motto was, "Come as you are, life ain't nothing but a party," and he meant it. Half of the time he didn't have anything on underneath the giant white fur coat he used to wear everywhere.

As carefree as he could be, though, George could also get very serious. The band was booked to do a show at an air force base in late 1976 or early 1977, shortly after the end of the Vietnam War. His music was really popular with the young soldiers, and we'd been hired to come out and play a big outdoor event. At the time I was musical director, so I was offstage more than I was on. Things went pretty well until about midway through the third tune, when one of the officers in charge of handling the band came to me and informed me that a high-ranking general—the base commander, in fact—was there with his family that night. The officer was concerned about the level of profanity in the show and asked me if I would ask George to tone it down for the rest of the night. I laughed out loud and just shook my head.

"I will convey the message," I assured him, and the next time George came offstage for a second, I did.

"What?" he yelled. "Man, eff him! They knew who we were when they sent for us," he said.

I knew he had no intention of toning down anything, but what I wasn't prepared for was the complete onslaught of profanity and vulgarity he let loose after that. He marched right back out to that microphone and let loose like I'd never heard before. It was really over the top, even for George. He let the air force base commander know he wasn't about to censor the show for his or anyone else's benefit. The air force got what they paid for that day.

For all of the insanity, there were some really profound moments that I'm glad to have been a part of. The first big tour I did with them was the P-Funk Earth Tour in 1976, which followed the release of *The Mothership Connection*. George's concept was that we were all from outer space and our mission was to come to Earth to show everyone what funk was all about. (I've always thought this was a noble cause.) To make his ideas come alive, George had devised an incredibly elaborate stage setup designed to shock the audience, pull them into the illusion, and bring them along for the ride.

Rock bands had been using pyrotechnics and massive stage designs for years, but this was something entirely new to funk audiences. The first time I saw "the Mothership" land onstage and watched George emerge from that thing was every bit as impressive and awe-inspiring as any of James's electrifying spins, twirls, and splits. At one show the prop guy in charge of setting up all the effects packed too much explosive powder into the charges, and when they went off during the show, the concussion shattered all of the windows in the building. What was strange to me was the reaction of the people in the audience who were cut by all the falling glass. They were actually *proud* that they'd been injured, wearing their cuts like badges of honor.

The shows went like this: after the opening act and Bootsy's Rubber Band played, Parliament-Funkadelic would hit the stage without George and warm up the crowd for a while. When the signal was given during "Star Child," Glen Goins would shield his eyes from the lights and look out beyond the crowd. "I think I see the Mothership coming," he'd start singing. The crowd knew this refrain meant George was about to arrive and would go absolutely crazy. The band would come in and sing the backup part—"Swing down sweet chariot, stop and let me ride"—and Glen would really pick it up and take it to a spiritual place with his voice, which he learned to do by singing in the church during his childhood. "I think I see the Mothership coming. Over there!" (Glen died of lymphoma in the late 1970s, but knowing him was one of the true pleasures of working in that band.)

Once the crowd reached a deafening roar, sparks would start shooting off way at the back of the auditorium and a tiny spaceship began descending over the crowd, making its way toward the stage. It was only a tiny model guided in by a wire, but it got the crowd's attention. The wire was attached to the underside of a large 1970s-style floppy cap with a pair of sunglasses stuck in the front. The ship flew down and eventually stopped underneath the cap, out of the view of the audience. Inside the cap, though, was a life-sized, hollowed-out version of the ship that could be lowered down onto the stage.

While the crowd was distracted by the ship overhead, George was wheeled out on a hydraulic lift that had steps running down the front to the stage. There was so much smoke onstage that no one in the band, let alone anyone in the audience, could really see this happening. Once the tiny ship was safely underneath the cap, lights and sparks would shoot out all over the stage from the underside of the larger version of the Mothership as it lowered itself down directly on top of the riser. It was all constructed so that it fit perfectly over the stairs hidden by the fog and the shower of sparks. When the door to the ship opened, light hit the front of the ship and it looked like the stairs had been lowered. George would be pushed up on the lift and emerge from the open door in a floor-length white fur robe and matching hat. He'd walk down the stairs to the stage looking like he'd just arrived from some distant planet. People went absolutely insane for this.

As awe-inspiring as all of the spectacular sets and lights were, I thought that the show itself was still lacking something. One of the reasons that the arrival of George in the Mothership was so impressive was that no one really knew who anyone else in the band was. To the crowd they were just an army of crazy-looking people onstage surrounding the star of the show. The show needed an emcee, someone who would introduce the band, announce the soloists, and engage the crowd during the warm-up vamp before George hit the stage. This loosely organized chaos needed a little more organization.

I'd been emceeing the James Brown show for years, so I took it upon myself to come up with a little introduction at the start of the show. I announced the band members, talked to the crowd, and directed things until it was time for Glen to announce the arrival of the Mothership. George appreciated it and eventually gave me the go-ahead to direct things as I saw fit, to a degree. I was still expected to play at some point each night—after all, George didn't hire me on as a stagehand. Ultimately I had the freedom to play when I felt like playing, even if it was just a cowbell some nights. This freedom to do what I liked was a bit of a contradiction given all of the organization I was preaching, but I felt like it was a benefit due me for having taken the initiative in the first place. After a while I took this initiative one step further and started to add a little direction to the stage show as well. People were used to just wandering on- and offstage as they wanted, but I became something of a stage manager and directed people. I knew who had a solo and when and would hurry them out onstage when it was time, then wander back out and collect them when it was time to come off. I became the organizational counterpoint to George's free spirit. He was the good cop and I was the bad cop, armed with a clipboard.

This "new sheriff in town" approach didn't go over so well with everyone, though. There were always people hanging around; if fifteen people were onstage, twice as many were backstage and even more were at the hotel. One trumpet player (who shall remain nameless) liked to come around whenever we were in L.A. and sit in, which was always fine with George. The guy would usually show up with an entourage of his own, which was also fine. One night onstage, as I walked around with my clipboard, sending people off and bringing people on, this guy snatched it out of my hand. *Whap!*

"Gimme that damn clipboard," he shouted, grabbing the thing from me as he proceeded to mock what I was doing.

Unlike my brother Melvin, I don't generally have a bad temper, but I felt a surge of anger come up inside that made my teeth grind. This guy's back was to me, and I saw a tiny TV screen appear on the back of his head. In this TV, I could see two seconds into the future, and there, on the screen, I saw myself cock back and punch this guy right in the back of his skull. Luckily for him I heard my mother's voice telling me to calm down, that I had to represent my family respectfully, so instead I gently took my clipboard back and went on about my business. I was pretty angry, but I wasn't going to hit this guy onstage.

Backstage I was still seething. The band's massive security guard, Brim—a former Oakland Raiders football player—could tell I was upset and asked me what was wrong, so I told him the story. We laughed about it and just shook our heads.

"I'll take care of it," he told me, and instantly I felt sorry for this trumpet player.

After the show, I'd completely forgotten about the whole thing and made my way to the hotel. P-Funk afterparties are legendary, so I don't think I need to go into all of that, but it's enough to say that there were quite a few people partying and carrying on that night on our floor. I decided to get some air and started down the hall to the elevator, where Brim was standing guard in front of the doors making sure only invited guests came up.

Just as I got to where he was standing the doors of the elevator opened, and there was this guy from before, surrounded by three or four women. All of them looked pretty messed up already but were coming up to do some partying with the band, apparently. Brim looked at me, looked back at this guy, and without a word reached into the elevator and grabbed him by his throat. With one motion he lifted this guy *off his feet* and slammed him into the wall outside of the elevator.

"Don't you *ever* mess with Maceo again! You hear me?"

It was one of the most frightening things I've ever seen, and this guy's face went completely pale. None of the ladies got off the elevator, and after a tense second the elevator doors dinged shut and they went back down to the lobby. I don't think they ever made it back up to meet the band that night. I was so scared I kept walking past without looking. When I turned the corner Brim still had this guy by the throat up against that wall. When I think about that I still get a good laugh. I'm pretty sure that guy never spoke another word to me.

It might seem odd that someone who never drank or took drugs in his life could be involved with a band with so many excesses. But my concept was never to get into anyone's business after the show. I was busy enough telling them what to do onstage. I looked the other way and withdrew from that scene until it was time to get onstage again.

This new direction that I'd brought in had the added benefit of saving George some money. Concert promoters have to hire all of the sound and lighting engineers and the enormous crew that it takes to set up the gear and stage props, then tear it all down when the show is finished. Getting the stage set up and then dismantled in a timely fashion is a lot of work, and for our set it took a small army of guys to do it, considering that the sets arrived in six or seven trucks each night. All of these guys were union workers, and if they worked one minute past their allotted time they got paid a whole lot extra for the overtime. That extra money came out of George's pocket, not the promoter's, so it was really important to end the show at eleven if the show was supposed to end at eleven—not eleven-fifteen, not twelve-thirty or one.

During a show, though, the *farthest* thing from George's mind was ending on time, so I worked out a signal with the road manager to tell me when it was time to wrap things up. When I got that signal I would casually let George know one way or another that it was time to wind it down. If I couldn't get his attention I would just conduct the band out of the song, and that would be the end of it . . . usually. If he was really feeling it George would wave me off or start up another song after we'd already stopped the show, and we'd play past our time. For the most part it was a good system and usually worked out well for everyone. Everyone except for the union guys, that is.

By the time we started playing "Atomic Dog" in the eighties, George had reached some kind of cult status. A fraternity, Omega Psi Phi, whose members called each other "Q-Dawg," used that song as their anthem. It was crazy.

Later on I started playing with Bootsy's band more and more. He was a little more concerned with uniformity when it came to dress, so the band usually wore some kind of matching, tight-fitting Lycra outfits. Outfits like that were part of Bootsy's concept, so I wore what the band was supposed to wear.

"Mudbone" Cooper used to do the real high, almost falsetto singing for Bootsy. His given name is Gary, and I used to joke with him that his parents must not have been able to think of a name when he was born, and sitting beside the crib must have been a *TV Guide* with a Gary Cooper movie listed. All joking aside, I really enjoyed working with Gary, and whenever I'm near Paris I always call him up to see if he's available to sing with my band. I love it when people enjoy working with me to the point that they tell me to call them up if I ever need them.

Those really were the fun years. Sometimes, though, I feel like it was a waste of time musically. It's hard for me to say that, but it's true. I can't say that during this time I learned how to voice horns, for example. I didn't grow as a musician. I had a lot of fun and wouldn't change any of it if I had it to do again (probably), but I really didn't grow musically during this period in my life.

In other words, I had already been established from the James Brown thing as "Maceo," and being part of this band didn't further my ambitions as an artist. The record company idea that brought me on board in the first place never materialized, and I didn't make any strides toward achieving my dream of having my own band. Every so often, in the midst of all the fun and chaos, I would look at my watch and see the seconds of my life ticking away. I knew my time with Bootsy and George would be short because I could hear myself saying, "You'd better get on with doing *your* thing if you're ever going to do it." I'm not blaming anyone but myself for putting my career on hold. I really should have started putting my own thing together. But I was having fun, and that—and gaining a really close friend in George Clinton—is the real legacy I'm left with from this time.

9

The Lean Years

Returning to the James Brown Band in 1984 was a purely economic decision. I knew I wasn't going to get anywhere with my solo career by going back, but at least I knew I could count on a steady paycheck while I figured out some things. James was experiencing something of a comeback in the early eighties; his appearance in the movie *The Blues Brothers* as well as a few shows in Beverly Hills at which Prince and Michael Jackson made guest appearances helped introduce him to a younger audience. After a rough patch in the late seventies, he was touring successfully in America again, and I thought it would be a good time to rejoin the band while I worked out how I could get my thing going. It didn't take me long to realize that things were very different from when I'd left a decade earlier.

James had been having problems with the IRS for years, but they had gotten especially bad. The stress of fighting them and relentless touring had taken its toll. He just didn't seem healthy. The band wasn't right. James had always surrounded himself with great musicians, and I was shocked to see the caliber of players he had with him now. Drug use was rampant and was responsible in large part for the decline in the musicianship. Even more shocking was how out-in-the-open it was. These new cats weren't even trying to hide it. Neither was James, for that matter. When Melvin and I first joined the group, a few cats would have a little to drink on our off days or during a particularly long bus trip. They might have gotten a little loud, but there was always a limit. This time around, though, the hard drug use created a division between those who did and those who didn't. Moreover, the ones who did fought about who owed whom for something they'd snorted the night before or who'd spilled someone's stuff on the hotel carpet. All the love, support, and unity—the DNA of those early bands—was clearly gone, and James didn't seem to care.

Some of these guys just couldn't play. Period. It's no secret that George and a lot of the guys in Parliament used to be into some heavy stuff on a pretty regular basis, but even when they were messed up those guys could play well. This wasn't the case with James's new group, which made it really difficult to get through some performances.

It was hard to believe that this James Brown was the same one I had known for the last two decades. The first impression is a lasting one. This man had preached pride, dignity, self-respect, and being a *man*. Most of that stuff was gone. He didn't seem to care, which made it incredibly difficult to be around him. Despite everything that had happened, James was still my friend. In a way, and perhaps naively, I thought that my presence could help him. I thought that if I were around him enough, maybe he'd remember the pride again and stop doing all of these crazy things. Unfortunately, I was wrong.

James just could not accept that getting older was a part of life. In his mind, he could do all the stuff he used to do in his prime— the spins, the splits, the turns and howls. But he couldn't do that anymore, and he just couldn't (or wouldn't) accept that about him-self. The musical world was changing in a big way as well. For a time there was no Michael Jackson or Prince to contend with, and James was the biggest name in show business. Now guys like them were out there really doing it, creating their own sound. *Purple Rain* was a huge hit in 1984, and I was really into it. Being an entertainer means that you're related to other entertainers—part of the same fraternity, so to speak. I've never felt that music was a competitive thing. But James didn't see it that way. I think it both-ered him that he wasn't the biggest name anymore. He especially envied Michael, although Michael had said publicly many times that James was his greatest inspiration.

Hip-hop was becoming hugely popular. I have always liked hip-hop and rap, although I do have a problem with the violent stuff that glorifies shooting and selling drugs. To me, rap feels like scat's funky cousin. The first person I ever heard rap was actually Kush when we were with All the King's Men back in the early sev-enties. He would mess around during rehearsals and rhyme silly lyrics to a beat, but we never took it seriously and certainly didn't record it. He was really good at making stuff up off the top of his head, but we just thought it was funny. James got on board with hip-hop in 1984, recording the song "Unity" with Afrika Bambaataa. The song was about "peace, unity, and having fun," something that I could relate to.

Despite the overall decline, there were some good times. One particularly bright spot was the movie *Rocky IV*. We were on set in Las Vegas at the MGM Grand for a week or so filming the sequence in which Carl Weathers's character, Apollo Creed, fights the giant Russian played by Dolph Lundgren. It was a bit of a chore having to remember exactly what we were wearing the day before or exactly where we were standing for continuity's sake, but it was a great experience nonetheless. Since the band on the set didn't actually record the song "Living in America," we had to learn the parts and mimic them for the movie, so in that sense we were actors in our own right, I suppose. I was really knocked out by the way that Carl Weathers could move around that ring. He was light on his feet, dancing around just like Muhammad Ali. He really made it look convincing.

It was an odd experience being on such an elaborate stage set with James since his shows weren't anything like that anymore, although it reminded me of a time when he played Vegas years back. Still, having James and the band fit the movie perfectly. The whole idea was that Apollo Creed wanted to give this young Russian upstart a real piece of America, and how much more American can you get than James Brown?

Another great time was around 1987 when we were playing the Apollo Theater (again). The show started off with the emcee announcing, "Now ladies and gentleman, the James Brown Show!" and—*bam*—we were off into it. I don't remember what we were playing, but it began with my solo right off the bat. I started playing, walking around the stage for a bit, when I got the funny idea to walk down into the audience. People went crazy, so I went with it. I walked up and down the aisles just playing and playing. At some point I saw this couple sitting near the aisle. I don't know what made me decide to do it, but I decided to play to just them. Exclusively. As I got to where they were sitting, I motioned for the lady, who was seated on the aisle seat, to stand up as if I wanted to dance with her. In the middle of this commotion, I realized that it would be funnier if I left her in the aisle and took her seat. I just sat down. The place went crazy.

This woman was dancing and doing her own thing, completely unaware that I was occupying her seat. Her date, who was now seated next to me, absolutely *loved* it. I mean he was having a ball. Once she finally realized that I was in her seat and not dancing, she started laughing as well. It was hilarious—she was finally in on the joke the entire theater had been laughing about. After the moment was over I politely got up and made my way back to the stage, the crowd completely in the palm of our hands. It was time for the James Brown Show.

It wasn't until much later that I found out that the woman who'd stood up to dance with me was Jane Rose, the famous manager of Keith Richards of the Rolling Stones, and that the guy I was sitting next to—the crazy guy who'd been having such a ball—was Keith himself.

Several months later, as it turned out, I got a call that Keith wanted me to record on his solo album, *Talk Is Cheap*. I was a little nervous as I went to the studio that day, not because of the Apollo Theater incident, but because I had no idea what this cat *looked like*. I wouldn't have even known if he was there or not. I shook the hand of every English guy I walked up to in the studio acting like I knew who they were for fear that one of them might actually be Keith.

In between the gigs with James, I found time to do some other studio work as well. My association with George led me to do some recording on an album he was producing called *Freaky Styley* for a young funk group from L.A. called the Red Hot Chili Peppers. I had no idea how big they would later become. James recorded a couple albums during this time, *Gravity* and *James in the Jungle Groove*, which I was a part of. I did another recording for Bootsy's album *What's Bootsy Doin'?* in 1988. Later, my association with Bootsy led me to do a recording with an unknown club act named Deee-Lite. The single "Groove Is in the Heart" went to number one on the *Billboard* Dance Charts and featured Bootsy, me, and a rapper named Q-Tip from A Tribe Called Quest. I even made a small cameo in the video.

My main source of income at this time, though, was still touring with James Brown. Things went pretty well for a few years, but by the end of the eighties James's drug use had spiraled out of control. He became increasingly erratic and paranoid and even tighter with money than usual. The largest check I ever earned from him was for $8,000 for some recording I'd done. When I came to pick it up, he handed it to me but then cocked his head and asked me if I liked the Mercury Cougar he was driving at the time. It was a nice car, and I had on several occasions remarked that I really liked it, so I said, "Yes, Mr. Brown. That's a great car."

Before I knew what was happening happened, he snatched back the check and tossed me the keys, saying, "Well then, keep it. It's yours."

I couldn't believe what had just happened. It was a nice car, but it wasn't going to feed my family.

Things only got worse from there. James had a few scrapes with the law, which are well documented. In 1988, he was arrested for aggravated assault and failing to stop for a police officer, for which he was eventually sentenced to six years in prison. This arrest was the result of a problem that arose when some people attending an insurance seminar that was going on at a facility that adjoined his offices in Augusta used his restrooms. Reports were that James threatened some people with a gun, and when the police were called out, he fled in his pickup. The police chase that followed went across state lines and ended when the police shot out James's tires. When the dust settled James was in prison and I was out of work.

That incident effectively ended our working relationship. I never worked as a full-time member of his band after that. I'd already been away from the band for a few months when he went in, but his imprisonment meant that there wouldn't be any work with him at all for the foreseeable future. I was tired of my employment situation being subject to the ups and downs of someone else's crazy life.

In the winter of 1989, I had to start looking for other work to support my family. I was doing a lot of session work, almost as a freelancer. Bill Laswell was producing Bootsy Collins and running a lot of other recording sessions back then and would call me from time to time for session work.

One night before a session I was up really late and thinking about James being in prison when the words for a tune just popped into my head. I wrote down the words "let him out" and immediately thought of someone like Bobby Byrd doing a call-and-response phrase like on "Get Up." Then a little rap part came to me that went, "Hey, Judge, it ain't funny. Let the man out so we can make money. His time is up, he's made the grade. Let the man out so we can get paid." The more I started writing lyrics down, the more they came to me. "Come on, Judge! You weren't there, you didn't see it. Whatever he did, he didn't mean it. Hey, Judge! Don't be a jerk. Let him out so we can go to work." By the time I was ready to go to bed at about four o'clock in the morning, I had almost the entire song written out.

During one of the sessions, I approached Bootsy and showed him what I'd come up with. He really liked what I'd written and started incorporating it into something we were working on. Eventually it became its own song. We listened back to it at the end of the recording session and it sounded great, almost perfect, just the way it was. I was really encouraged and thought to myself that the song had the potential to really be popular when it was released. Fred, Bootsy, and I actually performed "Let Him Out" on *Late Night with David Letterman* with Paul Shaffer and the show's band one night. It was a really tight performance full of that James Brown–style funk groove, which is what the song was supposed to have. When I finally heard the recording on the record many months later, though, it was all wrong. All kinds of violin and other string parts had been recorded over the top. Every bit of *funk* had been choked out of the song. I wanted that raw James Brown type of feel, but what ended up on the final recording was more of a slick Phil Spector type of sound. I realize that bringing this tune to the studio at that time was a big mistake because it was treated as a joke. I know that if it had been produced properly it could have been a big hit.

Still, the recording session was work, and I certainly needed the money. Things were very hard for my family, which, with the addition of my youngest daughter, Kendra, was now at eight. My brother, DeLond, had a good job with UPS at the time, and I routinely had to ask him for twenty dollars here and fifty dollars there just to make ends meet. The eight of us were crammed into a small three-bedroom house in Kinston and, even after converting the garage into another bedroom, we couldn't escape the fact that we just needed a much bigger house. As work ebbed and flowed so did the money, and there was a time when we fell behind on our rent for about five or six months. As bad as things were, though, I could feel a change coming. Something big was on the horizon, and I knew things would improve soon. Luckily our landlady was a kind woman who was good enough to see how we were struggling and gave our family some breathing room. When the work started picking up again, I was able to pay her the back rent and give DeLond the money I'd borrowed.

During this period, I would answer every call and go into the studio to record for just about anybody who was offering me work. My friend Vince Henry, a session player in New York who'd done some work with Whitney Houston, would throw some studio work my way whenever he could. Vince would call around and find sessions for me or, if he was unavailable, recommend me to the producer. Sometimes he shared a session he'd already booked for himself because he knew how badly I needed the work. (Vince and I are great friends, and when he and his wife had their first child, they named him Maceo, which I'm very proud of.)

Another time, Fred and I were hired to go to the studio and told to "just play." No specific key, no real melody in mind—just play. A few months later, we saw the CD marketed as horn samples to be used in hip-hop tracks. We were furious, because packaging our music like this was never discussed during the session. I had been reduced to recording samples for any "producer" who had enough money to go buy a CD with my sound on it. These were tough times, though, and I did what I had to in order to keep food on the table and pay the bills. Still, it made me think about what sampling was doing to musicians. James Brown is probably one of the most sampled artists in hip-hop, but for many years it was legal to "borrow" funk hooks from his records and make larger works out of them. "Soul Power '74" has been used several times. The artists who recorded these eventual "samples" were very rarely credited and almost never paid. I really respect De La Soul who, rather than sample a bunch of funk records, actually brought my band (which included Fred and Pee Wee) into the studio to record a few tracks on their album *Buhloone Mindstate*.

Around this time, a court case was brought by the French publisher of "Southwick" from the original Maceo and All the King's Men album, *Doing Their Own Thing*, against a comedian who'd used a sample from the song without permission. The comedian's lawyers actually argued in court that he'd made the recording *better* by what he'd added to our track. After several years of litigation, though, the French courts decided that he was in violation of the law, and eventually the band was compensated for the use of our work (as was the publisher, who owned the rights to the song). I don't remember it being a lot of money, but it was the moral victory that was more important to me. Respect artists, respect their work, and if you intend to use it, compensate them fairly.

Things turned a corner for me in 1989 when I got the offer to tour Europe as part of a James Brown tribute show organized by Bobby Byrd that featured an all-star cast of James's associates, including Marva Whitney, Martha High, Vicki Anderson, Lyn Collins, and most important, Pee Wee and Fred. It was a brief tour that produced some amazing shows performed to sold-out crowds excited about hearing the classic James Brown tunes again. I guess his incarceration created a buzz overseas, and people were clamoring for that sound. As performers we were paid well, but Pee Wee, Fred, and I realized there was a real opportunity for us if we could do our own tour when Bobby Byrd's James Brown tribute tour was over.

Fred and I discussed doing a kind of Sam and Dave thing, but before any of that materialized, a friend of Pee Wee's, a guy by the name of Jim Payne, asked the three of us to come out to a studio in Florida to record for him. Jim was a drummer, and the idea was to work out ideas on the spot and release a disc in order to get some gigs as the J.B. Horns. From the outset I knew I needed to do it, but my heart was still into getting a strictly solo project off the ground.

Working with Pee Wee and Fred was magical; we have a kind of energy together that I don't think will ever be duplicated, and I will always love those guys. But as successful as the J.B. Horns recording and shows were, our concepts have always been very different, and at the end of the day the project felt like a compromise in one way or another. I wasn't getting any younger, and every day that I postponed working on my own music I could feel this dream slipping further and further away from me. After all the time I'd spent in this business, I began to look around and see people with less experience and nowhere near the clout that I had making it big. I was just scratching the surface. I knew that the next step I needed to take in my career was to have my own band.

The concept and the desire were there, but I ran into that familiar stumbling block of not knowing exactly how to get things off the ground. I knew what I didn't want to do, though. I didn't want to record some tunes and then try to shop them around to different record labels. Instead I wanted a record label to come to me. I felt that approaching a record label with my material meant that I had to listen to what they had to say. If, on the other hand, a record label or a producer were to approach me, I knew they would have to listen to my ideas.

A German producer named Stephan Meyner finally approached me about recording a solo album. Stephan had been working with another producer named Giancarlo Duilio and had recorded one of the shows on the Bobby Byrd tour in Europe. Stephan spoke a fair bit of English and we developed a real rapport over the phone, discussing ideas for an album. He was open to my concepts, but he had his own ideas that I had to come around to. He was a real jazz lover and had this vision of recording my funky sound in a different context. Ultimately he wanted to make a funky jazz record with heavy swing and blues influences.

"Everyone knows you can play funk," he told me, "so why don't we do a jazz record? Nothing really heavy or out, but just put some real *swing* in there."

The idea sounded interesting to me, and before long I was on a plane to Germany to record an album that would later be titled

Roots Revisited, a title that acknowledges the record's mission to revisit funk's roots in jazz and blues.

I called up Fred and Pee Wee and asked them to record the album with me, which they agreed to do. Along with the amazing organ player Don Pullen, who used to play with Charles Mingus, Bill Stewart on drums, and Rodney Jones on the guitar, we had a really tight band. The music was complex with a lot of changes and honestly wasn't exactly what I had in mind, but it gave me the chance to record my own compositions, like "Up and Down East Street," a nod to the place in Kinston where I first began to gig with my brothers, and "Children's World." In time, I knew I'd be able to record something more in line with what my concepts were, but at that time I felt like I needed to get this thing off the ground, and recording *Roots Revisited* was a big step toward beginning the solo career I'd waited for so long to start. Everything I had done to this point—all the years on the road, all the time on the sidelines, all the struggling and scratching—hadn't been in vain because I was finally getting somewhere. The release of this record marked a new beginning.

10

A Funky Renaissance

Roots Revisited became a very successful record and spent ten weeks at the top of the Billboard jazz charts. I followed that up with another successful recording in 1991, a year later, called *Mo' Roots*, which also featured Pee Wee and Fred and was produced by Stephan again. The success of the recordings meant gigs were coming in right and left and we were making money—our *own money*. We were billed as Maceo Parker Featuring Fred Wesley and Pee Wee Ellis, names that promoters felt would get the greatest recognition. It felt great to be in the driver's seat for a change rather than relying on James, George, Bootsy, or anyone else for an income. But I still had the feeling I was missing something. As good as things were, I wasn't exactly where I wanted to be yet.

That nagging feeling of being directionless and just treading water didn't subside until I met my manager, Natasha Maddison. I was very lucky to run across someone like her. She is incredibly gifted at organization and management. She has the ability to identify a goal and plan out the steps necessary to achieve it. Even more important, she then follows through and makes things happen.

When I met her, Natasha was working for a management company out of London. We were starting to get gigs across Europe fairly regularly with a lot of success. The money we were making was good and getting better, but we involved ourselves with another booking agent in New York for gigs stateside. What drew us to the London company was the promise that they could find royalties owed to us from past work, which sounded great to us. Their position was that since they didn't formally represent us as management, they couldn't act on our behalf in pursuing these royalties. They wanted us to come on board with them in some sort of management deal, and I wasn't sold on that type of arrangement. I just didn't have a good feeling about the whole thing.

Natasha and I discussed the situation one evening, and I told her about my misgivings about our current booking agencies. Eventually I told her about the dream of having my own group and explained to her what my concept was. I tried to lay out as clearly as I could what I envisioned this group could be—all of the things I wanted my group to do musically. I didn't want to go too much over the top with a show, but I wanted to develop something more than the standard round-robin format for solos, the kind of show where everyone takes a turn on every single song and the only thing that really changes night after night is the order of the soloists. I wanted a Maceo show to be about interaction and spontaneity. Most of all I wanted my thing to be about spreading love in the world.

Natasha completely understood where I wanted go and knew what it would take to get me there. In a very short time, we developed a real bond of friendship and respect. She told me that the London company wasn't being up front with us about what we were being offered for the shows they were booking and was keeping a little more for themselves than they probably should have been. This didn't come as a huge shock, but in telling me what was going on she was letting me know that I could trust her to work honestly on my behalf. After our talk I felt confident that she was the person who could really help me get this Maceo thing off the ground. For the first time I had a real sense that my dream of having my own group—doing my own thing—was finally within reach. I'd found that missing piece.

At our next meeting at the booking agency I told everyone that Natasha Maddison now represented me as my personal manager and they would have to deal with her when it came to my affairs. Successful musicians always had great management—James had Ben Bart, Elvis Presley had Colonel Tom Parker—and I now had someone in my corner. That decision turned out to be one of the best I've ever made. Natasha and I have conquered a lot of ground together over the years, and I've never looked back. Fred and Pee Wee backed my decision. Before long we saw our share of the revenue, as well as the number of gigs, increase considerably.

In 1992, we recorded a live show in Cologne, Germany, which became my bestselling record, *Life on Planet Groove*. I was still involved with Stephan Meyner, but the music we were playing at the shows had gotten away from the jazzy thing he'd envisioned and was more in line with what I did best—playing the funky stuff. We did James's "I Feel Good" and a new rendition of "Soul Power '74," which was renamed "Soul Power '92," as well as my own composition, "Got to Get'cha," which I'd previously recorded with the King's Men. The big hit from the record, though, was "Pass the Peas," a song that would eventually become something of a calling card for me. Larry Goldings, on Hammond organ, played an incredible solo on that song. In the middle of it, I got the crowd involved by shouting, "Go Larry! Go Larry! Go!" (Oddly enough, some sportscasters quote this phrase when referring to the NFL wide receiver Larry Fitzgerald, and it is something of an unofficial chant for him these days.)

The album opened up some doors that I hadn't seen before. Funky music was popular with a whole new group of people who were too young to be there for the James Brown thing but probably heard this music from their parents or sampled in hip-hop. One artist who went out of his way to acknowledge James Brown's influence on hip-hop was MC Hammer, who was one of the biggest stars in the world.

A month after leaving prison in February 1991, James Brown flew out to Oakland to tape an HBO special with MC Hammer titled *Influences*. The premise was that an older, established performer would interact with a young, up-and-coming artist. The show was supposed to document them talking about music, their influences, and what they admired about each other; eventually they were supposed to perform together. James was worried that he wouldn't be able to get everything together in time with a completely new band, but the producers of the show had thought of everything and had already flown Pee Wee, Fred, and me out to California to do the rehearsals and taping. I know James was relieved to hear that news and was genuinely happy to see us there at the first rehearsal. Because we were there I think he was able to relax and enjoy the show a little more.

MC Hammer had this huge band full of young musicians, and I remember laughing with Fred at how shiny their horns were. They looked like they might have had the price tags from the music store still hanging on them. It was a strange gig, but James looked good alongside Hammer and the wonderful gospel singer Tramaine Hawkins. Hammer came out and rapped and danced on "Cold Sweat," and it was pretty obvious that he'd studied James Brown. I think he had a genuine appreciation for the man. James was just grateful to be out of prison and performing again. After the taping, it was back out on the road for Fred, Pee Wee, and me.

The makeup of the group changed in the early part of the nineties as the music we played became funkier. It was a natural progression. Our original guitarist, Rodney Jones, was eventually replaced by Bruno Speight. I knew Bruno from his time with the S.O.S. Band and had worked with him on the Bobby Byrd tour of Europe several years earlier. Bruno is really groovy and remains my guitar player to this day. When Bill Stewart left the group we had a lot of drummers come and go, including Melvin, who took a break from his teaching gig for a while to tour with us. Bruno eventually brought in Jamal Thomas, a guy he knew from the S.O.S. Band, who was a perfect fit for us. Jamal stayed with me for many years until he got his own group in Europe, which led me to hire Melvin's son, Marcus. Marcus had a bit of a rough start but is now close to perfect, and I love having him in the band. Stephan Meyner introduced me to my current keyboard player, Will Boulware, who joined the band in the beginning but left for a while to do his own thing. Eventually Will returned to the band and is with me to this day. Another cat who came along was Rodney "Skeet" Curtis, one of the funkiest bass players in the world, whom I knew from his playing with George Clinton.

Fred and Pee Wee eventually moved on to do their own things, and I assembled a new horn section in their absence. I was fortunate to have Ron Tooley, one of the first people I met when I joined James's band, come on board with me and play trumpet, and a funky young guy from England, Dennis Rollins (who also has his own group), rounded things out on trombone. Martha High, another James Brown alum, joined the band as a vocalist. When we do the Lyn Collins song "Think (About It)," she really brings down the house. My son, Corey, also tours with the band from time to time. Slowly a nucleus of my own group formed—a group that could really play but that was also composed of people who I could get along with offstage. There are times when I stand back and look at the musicians around me onstage and feel an incredible swell of pride. These guys could play with whomever they want to, but for whatever reason they want to be part of my group.

Fred and Pee Wee leaving the band to pursue their individual interests was inevitable, and there is absolutely no ill will about that. I have an enormous amount of respect for them, and they will always be high on my list of people to love. When we play together it's magical, but at the end of the day we have different ideas and concepts about music. Their departure created a vacuum for a time, but it also created an environment in which I could really explore my own concepts and get into my own thing. The formation of the new incarnation of the band was a great awakening.

As much as my own thing was starting to take off, I still took some time to pursue other opportunities. In the midnineties, I had the pleasure of serving as musical director for the Rhythm and Blues Foundation's award ceremony for several years after having been in the show's band since its inception. The foundation's mission is to pay homage to important R&B, soul, gospel, and blues artists, many of whom have gone unrecognized for their accomplishments. It recognizes not only the "who's who" of music, but also those who once were but for some reason could no longer be. It reminds honorees that they haven't been forgotten and, in the presence of their peers, shows them how their influence has touched so many other artists. Those award shows were really something special.

Being recognized is one thing, but being *compensated* is something entirely different. Many of these people had never received any royalties for their work while they were active, so, in addition to all the recognition, they were also presented with a sizeable check (and I know some of them really needed the money more than the accolades). It was great to see some of these honorees accept their awards and for the first time get to say a few words about their work and their art. One night, Ernie K. Doe was given the Pioneer Award, and they could hardly get that guy off the stage. He was obviously overcome by the moment.

Even though some incredible hit makers like Stevie Wonder, Prince, and Gladys Knight were there, it never felt like the spotlight was on any one performer. It wasn't about "me," it was about "we." We had traveled the same roads and had similar experiences. We were there because we loved this music and wanted to lend our talents and time to a worthy cause, not to grab the spotlight. It wasn't like the feeling of friendly competitiveness when you're playing a festival and you want to outdo another band. The emphasis was always on the night itself and the appreciation for the talents that had brought us all into this odd fraternity.

Being backstage at the foundation's award shows felt a lot like a reunion. You would briefly run into many of these people when playing the same venues, but rarely for long. Most of the time there just wasn't an opportunity to talk. These shows gave you the chance to really catch up. It was like being around family you didn't get to see very often. It was also an opportunity to meet the people you'd always wanted to meet but maybe only knew through their music.

One evening backstage I felt a tap on the back and turned around to see Bubba Knight from the Pips standing there. He said hello and then mentioned that Gladys Knight wanted to meet me. All I could say was, "Wow." I was floored. On another occasion Eric Clapton awarded a check to the great bluesman John Lee Hooker and introduced himself to me right afterward.

"I've always wanted to meet you," he told me.

One thing I've always been self-assured and comfortable with is my place in the cosmos of musicians, but here at these award shows I found out just how many people I'd made an impression on.

My main duty as musical director was to lead the house band during the annual awards ceremony, which was much like the Grammys. It was an especially great job for me because I could sort of handpick guys for the band. People like Ry Cooder and Steve Cropper would come back almost every time because we had such a good time working together. One thing I really liked to do was try to come up with creative arrangements for the band to play, especially when someone had to walk up to the stage. I would check out the list of presenters and honorees during rehearsals and try to think up something creative to play as they came up. For Smokey Robinson, I worked in a little nod to "Baby Baby" as he came to the podium, for example. There were also performances during the evening, and I had to arrange and rehearse those tunes with the band. The same year Smokey Robinson was honored, Gloria Lynne was also an honoree, and we played her hit "I Wish You Love." Rodney Jones, who was part of my own band, played what is probably the prettiest guitar solo I have ever heard.

Another particularly meaningful night was the one in 1998 when I was asked to give an award to one of my idols, David "Fathead" Newman. To have finally realized my dream and be standing onstage with one of the men who'd inspired me to start this journey in the first place was overwhelming. Here was the man I'd seen perform some thirty-five years before, a man who I'd wanted desperately to someday know my name and know of my talent, and I was personally handing him an award for his achievements.

As with most things in life, though, you have to take the good with the bad. In 2003, I was awarded my own Pioneer Award from the Rhythm and Blues Foundation, along with George Clinton, KoKo Taylor, Dionne Warwick, The Supremes, and Jackie Wilson, among others. By this time, the foundation had grown considerably and was unfortunately spending a lot of its money on head-hunting musicians for the awards show. When the Pioneer Awards were handed out to that year's honorees, no checks were presented. I was no longer musical director at this time, but I'd been a part of the award shows for many years, and as far as I knew all of the previous honorees had received a check. It was explained to us after the show that the foundation just didn't have anything left that year. It was a bit of a slap in the face, and I wasn't the only one who thought so. Ray Benson, from Asleep at the Wheel, and Bonnie Raitt, the great blues singer and guitarist, were on the committee for the awards show and felt terrible about how things had turned out—so much so that they put on a charity event to raise money for that year's honorees. For that I'm truly grateful to them, because it showed how much they believed in the mission of the foundation, even if the foundation itself had lost sight of it to a degree. This incident was an unfortunate ending to a really wonderful chapter in my life.

In the early nineties, my oldest brother, Kellis, approached me about being a guest speaker at Columbia Law School. In 1972, Kellis had become the first black law professor at that university; now he wanted me to come speak to his students. He taught classes on contract law and gave lectures on the music industry, and he felt I could give these students some perspective on what a working musician has to deal with. I was apprehensive at first because I wasn't sure what I would say, but he kept picking at me until I finally agreed to do it. To my surprise the students were really fun to be around, and we had a really good time together. The talks were pretty informal. I told them about setting goals and achieving what you set out to do in life, and they asked me to tell stories about playing with James Brown. I had so much fun that I came back whenever my brother asked me to.

Kellis thought that I would make a good teacher and asked me once if I'd be interested in teaching a class on the history of funk.

It was an interesting idea. He told me I could arrange my own curriculum and devise the tests, but I'd decided long ago at A&T that I wasn't cut out to be a teacher. Kellis was Professor Parker. I was Maceo. Kellis did return the favor, though, by sitting in with our band from time to time on trombone. He kept up his playing through all the years of law school and teaching. His musical talents were passed down, and for about a year in 1996 his son, Kellis Jr., joined the band as a guitarist with his wife, Darliene, on vocals. (Kellis Jr. currently plays guitar with the very talented Janelle Monáe.)

Sadly, we lost Kellis Sr. in 2000. Unless you've lost a brother it's hard to describe the void it leaves in your life. He and Melvin are tied to my earliest and best memories; they are my oldest friends. I admired Kellis greatly, and I can't overstate the contribution he made not only to the law profession but to the cause of civil rights in this country and to the lives and careers of his students. I still miss him terribly.

One of the most profound moments in my life came in 1993. Natasha had gotten a call from George Wein's office at Festival Productions. They were putting together a winter tour that featured Ray Charles and were curious if I'd be interested in being the opening act. She already knew what my answer would be before she asked me: "Yes, yes, yes!" I was asked to tour all over Europe for four weeks with my idol, the man who towered above all other musical icons for me. Growing up I wanted nothing more than to be a part of his group. The men who played with him—Hank Crawford, "Fathead" Newman, Marcus Belgrave, Philip Guilbeau—were my idols, and I wondered how they kept their composure onstage every night around such a genius. His voice, his piano playing, and his songwriting were unlike anything I'd ever heard. I don't know where to put Ray on a scale of great jazz musicians like Cannonball Adderley, Stanley Turrentine, John Coltrane, or Charlie Parker, but I do know that earning a spot in Ray's band as a young man would have been enough for me.

People who weren't lucky enough to meet Ray might not know how funny the guy was. When he laughed, he would bend way over then rock back on his piano stool so far you thought he was about to fall off the thing. He also had a really filthy mouth, and he used to drop "motherf—er" in the middle of *everything*. I was backstage with him once when some people came up and asked for a photograph. They meant to ask if they could take a picture *with* Ray, but what they actually asked was, "Mr. Charles, do you mind taking a picture?"

"No, I don't mind," he said. "You're the one that's got to look at the motherf—er." I laughed so hard when I heard that I almost couldn't stop.

The night we played Paris during the tour the French promoter told Natasha that we should play longer than our allotted hour and a half because the French would riot otherwise. We had an especially great show. France has always been a special place for me and probably my biggest audience. Normally Ray arrived after we had finished our set but this night, because we were given extra time, Ray arrived before the end of the set and heard the crowd going wild. Natasha told me after the show that when he arrived and heard all the screaming, he said something like, "What's Maceo doing out there, taking his clothes off or something?"

When we got to Copenhagen, he told me he wanted me to come out and do a tune with him during his set. Not only was I touring with the man, but now I was being asked onstage to do a song together. I tried to play it cool, but that was almost too much. After the show that night I wanted to tell him how much that meant to me, but I was a little nervous and instead started talking about my horn. I'd heard stories about how well he could hear even the tiniest little flaw in your intonation, so I started to tell him how I tried to get everything perfect before coming out—I had to have a little "talk" with my horn.

"Yeah," he said. "I bet you said, 'Motherf—er, you'd better play good *tonight!*'"

I just cried. The man was so funny and engaging that I found myself wanting to be around him all the time; even though I was careful not to abuse the privilege of his company, I was completely fascinated by Ray. I tried to figure out how he and this tenor player he traveled with played chess with each other on the road. They had some kind of system worked out where Ray knew where all the pieces on the board were. It was really interesting to watch. I don't know if he got tired of my being back there as much as I was—I do remember he got onto me for "hollering too much" one time—but it was the thrill of a lifetime.

The real significance of the whole thing hit home for me that first night in Barcelona before the show. As I stood in the empty auditorium just before sound check, I couldn't take my eyes off the banner strung across the stage. It read, JVC PRESENTS MACEO PARKER AND RAY CHARLES IN CONCERT. I stood there for a long time taking it all in, realizing that it was *my name* up there next to Ray's.

Some thirty-five years later, I had made good on my promise to myself—Ray Charles *knew my name*. I realized that no matter what it took I had to have that banner, which was eventually given to me. It's sitting in my house to this day.

Someone called me about a year before Ray passed away and told me that he wasn't doing too well. I'd run into him at a show in Indiana about a year or two before his passing and chatted with him backstage for a while. I knew then that he was pretty frail, so this call wasn't a complete shock. Still, I wanted to call him up and find out how he was, but he and I were never close enough that I felt comfortable just calling up out of the blue like that. I wish that I had, though, because not long after that, he was gone.

It wasn't until several months after I heard Ray had died when the connection was finally made and the emotions came to the surface. It was while I was singing "Georgia on My Mind" onstage during my show. I started to get choked up and found it hard to sing. I couldn't figure out why it was hitting me now, all this time later. Somehow I was able to make it through. It still stings a little every time I do that song, though. Words escape me when I try to describe losing someone like Ray Charles. God bless you, Ray.

It was around this time, in 1993 and 1994, that I began to see a real sea change in the kind of audience I was attracting. I was hearing the same thing over and over after shows: "My friend so-and-so told me to come see you because he loved your show at Northwestern University," or "The campus radio station has been playing *Life on Planet Groove* all week." College kids were coming out in droves to see Maceo Parker where they could. But I wasn't always playing places that catered to them. In Boston, I was doing a few nights at a jazz club called Scullers, with a strict admittance policy of twenty-one and up, which meant a good majority of the local college students couldn't get in. (One manager in particular was very strict about allowing no dancing during the performance as well.) That first night scores of kids weren't admitted and were standing outside begging the door guy to let them in. Natasha and I realized that we needed to do something, so she persuaded the club management to open up the show to the adjoining hotel's ballroom and make it an all-ages show the following night. The show was a complete reversal of the night before and was full of college-aged kids who danced the entire time. It became clear that our audience had evolved from the sit-down, supper club jazz audience into a much younger, more vibrant crowd. Almost overnight our booking strategy changed. Natasha began to book the band in different types of clubs that catered to the college crowd, something that worked out very well for many years.

One byproduct of the new audience we were attracting was that the band got a little funkier. As we emerged from the staid environment of these jazz clubs and into larger clubs with dance floors, we had to beef up our sound a little. Up until this point Larry Goldings had covered bass parts on the Hammond organ. To fill things out and make our sound funkier, we brought in Jerry Preston on bass. The result was instantaneous—people were dancing and I was touring all over the country playing just about every night of the week. I could go just about anywhere, particularly in college towns, and pack a club on a Monday night.

Antone's in Austin was a good example of that. For years Clifford Antone (and later his sister Susan, who took over the club after his death) knew they could call us up and we'd be able to turn an otherwise slow week into two or three sold-out shows. The crowds there were out of control. At times I'd look up and see a line of girls dancing on the bar. One night a girl got on the stage somehow and started crawling on her hands and knees toward me while I was playing. I started slowly retreating, but this girl just kept coming right toward me, slinking her way across the stage like a cat until I was backed up against the wall and couldn't go any further. When she got to my feet, she just leaned her head down, kissed my boot, and then crawled back off of the stage. I had no idea if she was tipsy or if she was just so into the music that she just had to make a statement. It was strange, but in situations like that I'm always interested to see what people are going to do. Antone's has been really good to us over the years, and I have a lot of love for that place.

I've played a lot in Colorado over the years, and that place has been great to me, too. In 1994, I must have played every single club in the entire state. I played an old mining town once, a tiny little place called Rico, which has a population of about 250 people. I'm not exaggerating when I say almost every single one of those people came out to the show that night. Between 1994 and 1998, despite not having a new album out, I had an enormous response to the tours I was doing. This period was a real ground-building one, as I stretched out and reached a whole new crop of fans. The tours were almost nonstop then, and I did somewhere in the neighborhood of 250 shows a year. Word of mouth and the emergence of the Internet really helped expand my fan base and expose me to bigger and more diverse audiences.

In the later part of the decade, the shows got big enough that I was able to tour with all kinds of different opening acts, one of which was the ska/punk band Fishbone. They were really popular on college campuses at the time, but they could be pretty wild onstage, and their lyrics were laced with a good deal of profanity. When we got to Boston, however, the dean's office at Harvard approached Natasha and me and asked that anyone performing that night refrain from using profanity onstage. Fishbone wasn't their particular flavor, apparently. I could understand where they were coming from because my young daughters, LaShaun and Kendra, were on the road with me at that time. It wasn't just hordes of dancing coeds at the shows. The jazz crowd that had been with me since the beginning was still coming out, and many of them had children by this time. I started thinking about all the people who might be bringing their kids to a Maceo Parker show and the kind of experience I wanted *them* to have. I've worked with the likes of George Clinton, so it's not like I'm some prude, but I was becoming more conscious of what I wanted the entire experience of a Maceo Parker show to be—from beginning to end. I decided that anyone opening up for my band had to adhere to a strict rule of no profanity. I wanted anyone to be able to come to a Maceo show and feel comfortable. My next tour was with the great jazz/funk band Medeski Martin & Wood opening the show. They're an all-instrumental group—no problems there.

With Natasha's help, I steadily built my solo career up throughout the nineties. By 1998, I was opening up for some large acts with massive followings, like Dave Matthews Band. This tour excited my daughter LaShaun, who was really into them at the time. The band asked me to sit in with them after our opening set, and I told them I already knew four or five of their tunes just from hearing her playing their CD all the time.

In 1999, I had the pleasure of doing a tour with Ani DiFranco. I wasn't very familiar with her at first but found out later that she'd been coming incognito to my shows for years. Ani is a really sweet person, and after we met I noticed that she stood in the wings and watched almost our entire set that first night. I couldn't believe how happy she was to have me on the gig, and I was very taken with her personality. She reminded me of Candy Dulfer in a way—a really beautiful and gifted musician who was incredibly nice to be around. To this day it's still one of the best tours I've ever been on, both in terms of how the band was looked after and what a good time we had together. At a show in Vegas, Ani's band came out and did their entire set in shirts and ties, which was not their usual stage attire. They did this partly a joke since my band did dress up every night, but it was also a bit of an homage as well. They were having a little fun with us, and we found it pretty funny. One added bonus from this tour was meeting my eventual soundman, Goat. We reconnected in 2005, and he's been on the road with me ever since.

I got a lot of questions from the press during this time about the relationship between funk and folk. I sometimes like to describe music as a buffet where different musicians represent different kinds of flavors, each appealing to different tastes. We were playing a lot of large outdoor venues like Red Rocks in Colorado and Jones Beach in New York on this tour. There were usually large universities nearby, and it was interesting to see some of the younger hippie girls who were there who were embracing what we were doing. Night after night, they'd be there right in front of the stage dancing their hearts out.

While we were on this tour, both Ani and I received calls from Prince's assistant inviting us to come and record with him when we came through Minneapolis. When we did play there, Prince came, and the next day we went to meet him. (I'd actually met Prince briefly in 1991 while recording a piece for a British TV show. The comedian Lenny Henry had a program that documented different styles of music, and Fred, Pee Wee, and I, along with the band, had gone into Prince's Paisley Park studios to discuss funk and do some recording.)

Prince was recording the album that became *Rave Un2 the Joy Fantastic* and had written a tune he thought would be perfect for me called "Pretty Man," which is the hidden track on the album. I spent the afternoon recording the track, and afterward Ani, who'd already been there earlier in the day recording "I Love U, but I Don't Trust U Anymore," came back to the studio and we spent the rest of the time just jamming with the band. I can't say enough great things about Prince, so I'll just say this: the man is an absolute genius. I know that he doesn't really like for me to say that, but it's my book and I can say that if I want. He's a very private person, and it's important to respect that, so that's all I'll say. If you want to know more, listen to his music. I've had the honor of doing several tours with him since, including a stop at the 2004 Grammys, where he and Beyonce opened the show together. This performance also gave me the opportunity to work with another one of my favorite people, Candy Dulfer.

I first met Candy in 1991 when she recorded on my live album, *Life on Planet Groove*, and we've been friends ever since. We've done several tours together with Prince and recorded on each other's solo albums, including my *School's In*. She always stops by my shows when I'm in Holland and sits in, which really adds an extra-special element to the show; in 2010 she joined my tour as a "very special guest" for our Japanese dates. At one time she had a TV show in Holland called *Candy Meets*, in which she interviewed different musicians. She brought the show out to Kinston to interview me, and it was really great to show her around town, especially where I grew up in the Carver Court projects. We brought out our horns and jammed a little for some kids out on the basketball court there.

Paul Allen, cofounder of Microsoft, opened the EMP (Experience Music Project) Museum in Seattle in 2000, and I was asked to be a part of the Funk Blast exhibit. The exhibit included a short film designed to greet the visitors as they entered the museum and show them what funk was all about. As soon as you walked in you were transported to this wild block party where the entire neighborhood was dancing in the street and having a good time, watching James Brown and an all-star funk band of J.B. alums, including Bootsy, Fred, Bobby Byrd, and me. For the filming, they had me playing saxophone way up on one of the second-story balconies on the set. Natasha was worried I'd fall out of the little prop balcony they'd set up, so she had them strap me in with this uncomfortable harness. A young guy named Tony Wilson did the choreography for James during the shoot, wearing a bell-bottom suit and a rubber mask that made him look a little more like James. He was really good and pulled off the James Brown routine perfectly. The short film included some music we'd recorded for the exhibit that was produced by Marcus Miller. I was really impressed with what he put together.

My band was invited to play at the opening ceremony, along with Bootsy, Fred and the J.B.'s, and James and his band. It was an especially proud moment for me because I wasn't being asked to participate as part of James's band or Bootsy's band. I was asked to bring my band out and play.

I also released *Dial M-A-C-E-O* in 2000, an album that featured some great guest appearances—including Prince, Ani DiFranco, and a man I'd admired for a long time, James Taylor. Most of the recording was done in New York, and through my US record company I met James Taylor's daughter, who then introduced me to her father. I asked him if he would be part of *Dial* and told him that I would love to have him sing a little on the record.

"I can't really do any lead vocals," he told me, because of his recording contract. But he said, "I'd love to do some background stuff, though."

So we got in the booth and did this call-and-response thing on "My Baby Loves You," a song that I'd originally written to do with Dave Matthews, who couldn't be part of the album, unfortunately. James recorded some other backup harmonies to fill everything out, and as I listened to him singing I just couldn't stop grinning. James Taylor was in the studio recording something on *my* album. I'm eternally grateful for the luck that made it come together, because ultimately his singing makes that song come alive. We had so much fun doing the session that when he left he mentioned that he thought we should get together and do some writing sometime. That never happened, unfortunately, but I want to pay James back for doing that recording while I'm still able. (James, if you're reading this book, let me know if you have something funky for me to do with you sometime.)

There are opportunities that you seize and others that pass you by. Once while in Las Vegas with Prince I got word that Van Morrison was in town and wanted to have dinner with me. I'd worked with Van a few times over the years, so as soon as the show was over I met him at his hotel. I felt bad because I'd been held up after the gig and was running very late. He'd almost finished eating by the time I got there. Van really liked my work with James Brown and liked to do "Man's World" in his shows at the time.

"I've got a series of dates coming up, and I'd sure like to have you with us," he said.

He told me what the dates were, and I had other engagements with my band and just couldn't do it. I had to graciously decline, but I thought of another alto player who I thought would work and recommended him. Van was familiar with the guy and slammed his hand down on the table.

"Man, I don't *like* a saxophone player playing all those notes," he said.

I was a little surprised, but I knew what Van was talking about. He wanted my sound specifically. I was really flattered that he thought of me first and wished I could have made those dates work, because Van is a really great guy. Pee Wee was his arranger for a time, and Van would come by and sit in, usually to do "Man's World," when we were traveling in Europe in the early nineties.

In Europe, things developed for me in a different way: rather than playing a lot of university towns like I'd done in the United States, we started headlining a lot of the jazz festivals there in the late nineties, even though we weren't your typical jazz group. We drew a younger crowd that might not otherwise go to a jazz festival, and the promoters recognized that. We had some very successful tours and received a wonderful response from the crowds there, especially in France. I wanted to record another album, but the touring was so successful and I was gathering so much momentum that it was almost impossible to stop.

In 1998, I went to work with Joachim Becker, a German producer who worked with a more traditional jazz label. One of its big artists was Joe Zawinul, the great jazz keyboard player from Weather Report and the man who'd written one of my favorite songs, "Mercy Mercy Mercy." I really wanted to collaborate with him and knew it would be easier if we were on the same label. Unfortunately we never got the opportunity, although I did get to know him somewhat over the years. This really wonderful man encouraged me to sing more on my albums. In 2003, I had the honor of presenting him with an Amadeus Award, Austria's equivalent of a Grammy, for his album *Faces and Places*.

I ran into James Brown during one of these European tours at the North Sea Jazz Festival in Holland in 1995 I sat with him for a while and caught up. He was coherent again and looked healthier than I'd seen him in a long time. I got the sense that he recognized that I'd finally stopped "joking" about having my own thing and was taking care of business with my music. There was a different level of respect that came across that night, something I'd never gotten from the man before. We said our good-byes and my band went onstage after him. Things were perfect until a fire alarm went off right in the middle of our set. It was obvious after a few minutes that it was a malfunction and no one was in any danger, but Natasha was running around frantically backstage trying to get someone to turn the thing off. It was all but killing our set. I figured it would get shut off eventually, but I didn't want to lose the crowd in the meantime so I just found the note on my horn—a G—and started playing something funky in that key. The band caught on and fell in behind me with an improvised groove. The crowd loved it, and by the time the alarm was finally shut off, no one could even hear it anymore. People in the band were convinced that James had paid someone to sabotage our set, but I'm not sure. It was a little suspicious, but who knows? It might have just been an accident.

On Christmas Day 2006, I got the call to say that James had passed away. At first, I thought it was a joke. I really thought that James Brown would outlive us all. I *know* he didn't want to die—he was just that stubborn. I talked to Fred about it on the phone, and he was convinced that it wasn't true either, convinced it was a publicity stunt or something. I thought back on how James and I used to talk about doing three or four shows a year together when we got to be old men. "You know I'll make it worth your while," he used to say.

Ultimately, though, I had to make it pay for myself, and if I hadn't, what I'd done would never have amounted to anything. You can go through the whole roster of people who've played with James Brown and see what that association left them. For the most part, the answer is nothing. To come out from under James's shadow you had to have the vision to see where you wanted to go and the work ethic to accomplish getting there. I'm proud to say that I am one of a few who succeeded in doing that.

When I say that I had to make it pay for myself, I don't just mean monetarily. One of the great rewards of this job is the knowledge that I give something back. I was onstage one night at a club called Vega in Copenhagen when I noticed a woman in a wheelchair trying to make her way to the stage. She was at the far end of the room trying to maneuver between the people dancing, but she seemed to have this unstoppable sense of determination.

I couldn't help but follow her with my eyes while I played, and after a while she ended up at the far side of the stage. I lost sight of her but couldn't shake my curiosity about this woman. For some reason I had a feeling like I needed to find out what was going on with her, so after I finished my solo I stepped off the stage to see how she was doing.

I was pretty surprised to see that the woman was backstage in the wings talking to Natasha. Natasha introduced me to the woman and explained a bit of her situation. It was hard to hear, but I could make out that she had something important that she desperately wanted to say to the crowd. I trust Natasha's judgment completely and could tell that she was convinced by this woman's sincerity. Whatever she had to say was obviously important enough to fight her way through the crowd, so without another thought I brought her out after the song was over.

I lowered the microphone down, and she began to talk about a disease that had overtaken her, disabling and eventually completely crippling her body. She talked about the overpowering depression that set in as a result of being confined to the wheelchair.

"About a year ago I was suicidal," she told the crowd. "I thought very seriously about taking my own life, but luckily some friends took me to a Maceo Parker concert."

She explained to the crowd how embracing the positive vibe of the music that night lifted her spirits up and gave her a little break from the depression in her life. She explained how the message of love had made her think about the things she'd been contemplating. She talked about turning a corner in her life after that night and how since then she hadn't had any suicidal thoughts.

"I thought that was important enough to share with you all tonight," she said before thanking the crowd and quietly leaving the stage.

I'd always thought that it was important to not only play my music, but to spread a positive message of love where I went, and this woman's story was validation that what I was doing had made a real difference to someone. Artists sometimes get a bad rap because we take our work so seriously. It's not as if music is curing cancer. But the knowledge that my music had healed someone let me know that I was curing something else: loneliness and isolation, hatred and misery. I was adding love to balance out all of the negativity in the world. I decided right then that as long as I was going to tour and be in front of hundreds of people every night, I would talk about love as much as I could in my shows.

In 2011, I was inducted into the North Carolina Music Hall of Fame, which was a great honor. My name sits alongside music greats like John Coltrane, James Taylor, George Clinton, Ben E. King, Max Roach, Nina Simone, Roberta Flack, Billy "Crash" Craddock, Billy Taylor, and so many more.

I was honored in 2012 with a lifetime-achievement award from Les Victoires du Jazz. In France, this award is something like a Grammy, although, as you can guess by the title, it's specifically for jazz. I was proud to receive this award because it's indicative of how the French have taken me into their hearts over the years. We play more festivals and more shows in France than anywhere else in world.

It's an incredible feeling to retrace my steps. I've accomplished everything I set out to do and am intensely proud of the work I've done. I'm just another one of the keys on the keyboard of entertainers, another choice on the buffet of musicians, which is all I've ever wanted to be. And after nearly fifty years of playing music—from the Junior Blue Notes with my brothers to playing alongside James Brown and George Clinton to realizing my dream of having my own band—I can honestly say that I still love it. I love the people who come out to the shows and especially appreciate the fact that they get something out of our concerts. I throw "L-O-V-E" out there as much as possible because it's a concept that I still very much believe in. All of the traveling gives me the opportunity to spread my message of love throughout the world, which is why I still love to tour. I love my band. As long as I continue to enjoy doing all of the things involved in bringing a Maceo Parker show to the people night after night, you can bet that I'll be there giving as much as I possibly can, wherever I am.

Just show me where the stage is.

Index